I Cannot Be Defeated, And I Will Not Quit!

Taking the Future by Storm

I Cannot Be Defeated, And I Will Not Quit!

Taking the Future by Storm

Kenneth Hagin Jr.

Unless otherwise indicated, all Scripture quotations in this volume are from the *King James Version* of the Bible.

Scripture quotations marked NEW INTERNATIONAL VERSION are taken from *The Holy Bible, New International Version*. Copyright © 1978 by the Zondervan Bible Publishers, Grand Rapids, Michigan. Used by permission.

Excerpt taken from *It's Just a Thought But It Could Change Your Life*. Copyright 2001 by John C. Maxwell. Used by permission of RiverOak Publishing, Tulsa, OK. All rights reserved.

First Printing 2005

ISBN (paperback) 0-89276-746-4

In the U.S. write:
Kenneth Hagin Ministries
P.O. Box 50126
Tulsa, OK 74150-0126
1-888-28-FAITH
www.rhema.org

In Canada write:
Kenneth Hagin Ministries
P.O. Box 335, Station D,
Etobicoke (Toronto), Ontario
Canada, M9A 4X3

Copyright © 2001, 2005 RHEMA Bible Church
AKA Kenneth Hagin Ministries, Inc.
All Rights Reserved
First edition 2001
Paperback edition 2005
Printed in USA

The Faith Shield is a trademark of RHEMA Bible Church, AKA Kenneth Hagin Ministries, Inc., registered with the U.S. Patent and Trademark Office and therefore may not be duplicated.

Contents

Preface ix

1   Taking the Future by Storm 1

2   Living in Success 13

3   Tomorrow Begins Today 23

4   What Are You Looking At? 41

5   What Kind of Attitude Do You Have? 49

6   Set Your Sights 63

7   The Importance of Patience 71

8   Expect the Best 81

9   What Comes Out When the Pressure Is On? 93

10 Facing the Fire 103

11 Keep Striking the Ground 115

12 Possessing What Belongs to You 127

13 Stay in the 'Jericho March' 139

14 How to Succeed in Life 151

15 What to Do When You Don't Know What to Do 165

16 What Is Your Destiny? 173

Time flies. We've all heard that expression many times. What it means is that time passes quickly. This isn't just man's idea; the Bible says that this life on earth is "but a vapor." Because time passes so quickly, and because we are living in the last days before Jesus' return, it is vital that we make every moment count.

We need to live each day with everything we have in us—with our whole heart—and with a "never quit" attitude. My personal motto has always been "I cannot be defeated, and I will not quit." That is a good motto for anyone to live by—both naturally and spiritually speaking.

We have been made more than conquerors through Jesus Christ, and we can live victoriously in this life accomplishing all that God has for us to do. Instead of being worried about what the future holds, we need to take the future by storm!

I pray that by reading this book, you will learn to do just that!

Chapter 1

Taking the Future by Storm

This time, like all other times, is a very good one,

if we but know what to do with it.

Ralph Waldo Emerson

━━◆━━

In a "Peanuts" comic strip I read, Linus was talking with Charlie Brown about dreams and about the future. Linus said, "When I get big, I'm going to be a real fanatic."

Charlie Brown responded, "What are you going to be fanatical about, Linus?"

With an uncertain look on his face, Linus replied, "Oh, I don't know. It doesn't really matter. I'll be sort of a wishy-washy fanatic."

While that may sound funny in a cartoon, there's no such thing as a wishy-washy fanatic. And if we want to be successful as Christians, we can't be wishy-washy, either. If we want to take our future by storm—or to live victoriously in this life—we can't afford to be wishy-washy in what we believe or in the way we live.

One man who wasn't wishy-washy was Joshua, a great leader of Israel. Joshua was leading a group of people who were familiar with the price of being wishy-washy. The previous generation of Israelites had wanted to be delivered from Egypt's bondage. But after they were delivered, they began to complain to their leader Moses and say they wished they were back in Egypt. Because of their wishy-washy attitude, they wandered around in the wilderness for forty years and never entered the Promised Land.

But starting in Joshua chapter 1, we read about a generation of Israelites who were committed to taking their future.

JOSHUA 1:1–11 (*NIV*)

1 After the death of Moses the servant of the Lord, the Lord said to Joshua son of Nun, Moses' assistant:

2 "Moses my servant is dead. Now then, you and all these people, get ready to cross the Jordan River into the land I am about to give to them—to the Israelites.

3 I will give you every place where you set your foot, as I promised Moses.

4 Your territory will extend from the desert to Lebanon, and from the great river, the Euphrates—all the Hittite country—to the Great Sea on the west.

5 No one will be able to stand up against you all the days of your life. As I was with Moses, so I will be with you; I will never leave you nor forsake you.

6 "Be strong and courageous, because you will lead these people to inherit the land I swore to their forefathers to give them.

7 Be strong and very courageous. Be careful to obey all the law my servant Moses gave you; do not turn from it to the right or to the left, that you may be successful wherever you go.

8 Do not let this Book of the Law depart from your mouth; meditate on it day and night, so that you may be careful to do everything written in it. Then you will be prosperous and successful.

9 Have I not commanded you? Be strong and courageous. Do not be terrified; do not be discouraged, for the Lord your God will be with you wherever you go."

10 So Joshua ordered the officers of the people:

11 **"Go through the camp and tell the people, 'Get your**
supplies ready. Three days from now you will cross the
Jordan here to go in and take possession of the land
the Lord your God is giving you for your own.'"

With the Promised Land before them, it was no time for
the Israelites to be wishy-washy. And today, as we stand at the
brink of ushering in the Lord's return, it is no time for us to be
wishy-washy.

You see, this group of Israelites in Joshua chapter 1 had
stood at this same spot or close to it forty years before. It was a
dramatic scene.

In Numbers chapter 13, we read that Moses sent twelve
men to spy out Canaan, the Promised Land. Ten of the spies
came back afraid and said, "We can't take the land." They were
wishy-washy. Only two, Caleb and Joshua, came back in faith
and said, "Let us go at once and possess it, for we are well able
to overcome it."

The Price of Being Wishy-Washy

Unfortunately, many people are just like Linus in the Peanuts
cartoon in that they start to do something but they're wishy-
washy about it. In other words, they have the attitude that if
everything goes all right, then they will continue in their endeavor,
but if everything doesn't go all right, then they will quit.

We can't be successful in our Christian life with that kind
of wishy-washy attitude. If we're going to do something successfully, then we've got to make a commitment not only to start,
but to go all the way with it and see it through to completion.

In any endeavor, you will face some opposition. If you
haven't already made your commitment in advance, it will be
easy for you to quit when opposition comes against you.
Success requires complete commitment.

Studying the Book of Joshua, you will find that every incident comes back to this one principle: Obedience brought victory; disobedience brought defeat. Israel's commitment, or

obedience, to what God said brought them victory. Israel's disobedience to what God said brought them defeat.

Deliberate disobedience in Joshua chapter 7 brought a defeat at Ai. But complete commitment to obeying God in Joshua chapter 8 brought complete victory the next time Israel fought against Ai (see Joshua 8:1–28).

We need to have the kind of commitment that causes us to be fully devoted to God. Many people want to commit to God as long as they can reserve a portion of themselves for what they want to do. It doesn't work that way with God. God wants all of you—He wants you completely sold out to Him and His Word.

Referring to something in the Bible, someone might say, "Well, maybe God didn't mean it exactly that way." But if God didn't mean it, why did He say it? We need to have the attitude that if the Bible says it, we're going to believe it, and that settles it. We must be completely sold out to God in order to take the future. When you completely sell out to God, you release a flow of His power in your life that will take you through anything you face. God's power is available, and it's yours. But you can't be wishy-washy about it. You have to move out and do something about what God is saying to you.

A Second Chance

Referring back to Numbers chapter 13, Israel stood at the threshold of receiving what God had for them. But because of their fear, pessimism, and negativism, they were prevented from taking possession of the land that God had promised them. God had said, "It's yours," but because the Israelites were wishy-washy—because of their unbelief—they wandered in the wilderness for forty years. However, forty years later in Joshua chapter 1, the Israelites had an opportunity to recapture what their fathers lost.

It's not often in life that we get second chances. Sometimes, opportunities that people don't take due to fear, mistrust, or pessimism don't come around again.

But this new generation of Israelites who had come to maturity in the wilderness was given another chance to take the Promised Land. The word of the Lord came unto Joshua saying, "*. . . now therefore arise, go over this Jordan, thou, and all this people, unto the land which I do give to them, even to the children of Israel. Every place that the sole of your foot shall tread upon, that have I given unto you. . . *" (Joshua 1:2–3).

The challenge that was given to them to "arise and take possession of the land" isn't much different from the challenge that is facing us today. The Church of the Lord Jesus Christ—the *ecclesia*, the called-out ones—stands on the threshold of the Promised Land, so to speak. There has never been more openness to the Gospel than there is today. If you engage people in conversation, it seems you will always get around to talking about the things of God. We also see revivals breaking out in different parts of the world. Never before have we had such technology and tools to proclaim the Gospel message to the ends of the earth.

The time is right for a bold mission thrust. And just as Joshua told the Israelites, "Arise, go over the Jordan," God is saying to us today, "Arise, take My plan for your life. Take the plan I have for My Church. Arise to the challenge, go forth, and do what I've called you to do."

Of course, God wants us to do something that is useful in the day and age in which we live. Many times, so much of what is being done isn't very useful. A lot of time, energy, and money is being spent, but it isn't really helping anyone. We need to be sure that what we do is useful to others, ourselves, and to the Kingdom of God.

Let's study the children of Israel and learn some things that will be very beneficial to us as we embark upon our journey to take the future by storm.

Number One: Proper Preparation

Are you ready to take the future by storm? Are you ready to move forward and take what God has for you in your life?

Many people never fully embark upon life's journey because the future is a mystery to them which makes their path somewhat unknown. But even when we can't see our next step, we must be willing to walk into the unknown. The future is the unknown; no one knows exactly what lies ahead or what will happen tomorrow.

It's important to remember that even though you don't know what's in front of you, as long as you have planned and prepared, you can still succeed in life. The first thing we need in order to take the future by storm is *proper preparation.*

Most people who fail in life, even spiritually, fail due to a lack of preparation. If you read the whole Book of Joshua, you'll notice in the first three chapters that Joshua made some detailed plans before he and the people ever took their first step.

First, Joshua ordered that the Israelites prepare sufficient food. Second, Joshua sent spies into Jericho to spy out the land. Third, Joshua gave instructions to the priests and told them what they were supposed to do. Fourth, Joshua issued a challenge to the people (see Joshua 1–3).

Most people have to be challenged before they will respond. Well, I want to issue you a challenge today. We have a challenge before us today.

The world needs to be saved, and the saved need to be churched. The world needs to hear the Good News of Jesus Christ.

I've said it before, and I'll say it again: Government legislation isn't going to take away our problems. We're not going to be able to legislate poverty away. We're not going to legislate people getting along together. Jesus is the answer!

When a person has Jesus in his heart, he can discover the truth about all kinds of situations. For example, if a person's financial or employment condition is a result of his being sick, with Jesus in his heart and with the right kind of Word-based teaching, he now knows that he can be well. Once he is well, he will then be able to go out and make a living.

Also, with Jesus in our heart, the love of God is shed abroad in our heart by the Holy Ghost (Rom. 5:5). And we discover that people of all races and colors can sit down together, worship together, eat together, and fellowship together.

How to Prepare for Success

We need to make preparations if we're going to successfully do what God has planned for us to do in the future. First, we have to analyze the need. All you have to do is listen to a news broadcast, read a newspaper, or simply drive down the street, and you can see what the needs of society are.

Then before we move out to do something for Christ, whether it be to preach or do whatever it is we're to do, we need to prepare. For example, if you're to witness door-to-door, check out the neighborhood where you're going. In other words, pick out a target group. You may never be called to a five-fold ministry position, but as a member of the Church, you can go out and make a difference right where you are. You can get to know the people in your community, your workplace, your neighborhood, and so forth, and bring those people to God!

The next thing we must do to prepare is to assess our resources. What do you have personally to give to the Kingdom of God? Every church has resources found in its members. None of us is skilled at everything, but all of us, when we come together as a corporate body, have all the skills necessary to accomplish whatever we need to do.

In the RHEMA Bible Church congregation, there are master mechanics, attorneys, doctors, businessmen, bankers, teachers, construction workers, athletes, singers, instrumentalists, and so forth. You name the skill, and we have it at RHEMA Bible Church. What local churches need to do is gather their resources, target the people they can reach together, and do something for God!

Now let's do something about obeying God individually and pooling our resources to move out to take the future for God. We need to pray as if everything we're going to do in the future depends on God. Then we need to plan and execute the plan as if everything depends on us. It's the natural and the supernatural coming together that makes an explosive force for God!

Success is not all supernatural, and it's not all natural. Success comes by bringing your natural resources together with the supernatural resources from on High. When you put them together you become an explosive force for God, and something will take place that will benefit the Kingdom of God.

Number Two: Complete Commitment

Preparation is the first thing we need to take the future by storm. After we have made the proper preparation, we need complete commitment. God was not responsible for the Israelites taking the Promised Land. He told them He had given it to them, but whether or not Israel took the Promised Land was determined by the commitment they were willing to make.

If we are going to successfully do whatever God wants us to do, we've got to be committed to it. It takes the kind of commitment that says, "Sink or swim, come hell or high water, I'm going on with God!"

As I said before, my personal motto for life is, "I cannot be defeated, and I will not quit." That is the kind of attitude we as Christians need to have if we are going to take the future by storm.

My motto reminds me of a time I was wrestling with my uncle Pat. He had me in a hammerlock–holding my arm pinned behind me–and he kept saying, "Say 'uncle,' and I'll turn you loose." I told him, "Uncle Pat, you can break my arm, but I'm not going to say 'uncle.' Either turn me loose or break my arm so we can go to the hospital, but I'm not saying 'uncle.'"

That's what you call bull-dog tenacity! And that's the way I am. Don't tell me something can't be done. I believe there is always a way. For instance, when we were building the RHEMA Bible Church auditorium, I told the builders that I wanted a hole in the ceiling above the stage to hold a giant globe that would descend. I wanted the globe to come down out of the ceiling and rotate slowly, displaying lights on every city in which a RHEMA missionary is ministering. The building designers said, "We've never heard of anything like that. It's never been done that we know of."

I told them, "I don't care if it's never been done before. It can be done. Find out how to do it."

It took them a while, but they figured out how to do it. And now, during every Sunday morning service at RHEMA Bible Church, the globe descends and a light comes on to mark a particular location where a RHEMA missionary is ministering. Then we as a congregation pray for that missionary and that nation.

Number Three: Total Togetherness

So far, we've seen the roles proper preparation and complete commitment play in taking the future. The third thing we need is *total togetherness*. If you're going to accomplish anything as a natural family, and if the Body of Christ is going to accomplish something as a spiritual family, there must be total togetherness. In other words, you must be in unity. You cannot accomplish anything if one person wants one thing and another person wants something else.

Have you ever noticed that two horses hitched together are called a "team"? But, in effect, they are not a team if one horse pulls in one direction and the other horse pulls in a different direction. A team means all parties involved are pulling together with the same focus and with the same goal in mind.

This is what is wrong with a lot of families today. They're not living together in unity. While the dad does one thing, the mom and the kids are doing something else. If you're going to accomplish anything, you've got to be in harmony—you must have total togetherness.

The Power of Unity

Before Israel crossed the Jordan River, the tribes of Reuben and Gad and the half-tribe of Manasseh requested to stay on that side of Jordan and settle. Moses agreed on one condition—that the tribes of Reuben and Gad and the half-tribe of Manasseh go with the rest of the tribes and participate in taking the Promised Land. After the Promised Land was conquered the tribes of Reuben, Gad, and Manasseh would be allowed to go back to the other side of the Jordan and settle there. Moses realized that the task in front of them demanded the total efforts of all of the people uniting together. There is power in unity!

One of the reasons the United States Army is as strong as it is, is that they understand the definition and power of unity. They understand that if the highest-ranking officer falls in a time of battle, the person next highest in rank picks up the standard, so to speak, and carries on. Many of the United States' adversaries through the years have not been so unified, and when the person in command fell, the rest of the troops scattered.

I like to illustrate the power of unity this way: You can break one stick easily, but it is much harder to break several sticks bound together. We as Christians need to be bound together in unity as we move out to do the job that God has called us to do.

With the task that is before us, we must be willing to rise above "my way" and "your way" and do things God's way. There is my way, your way, and *God's* way. But when you're in God's army, you do it *God's* way!

I remember the time several new recruits and I piled off a bus at Fort Leonard Wood, Missouri, at two o'clock in the morning. A sergeant stood there shouting, "Boys, there's one thing I want you to know from the get-go, and that is this: There is your way, my way, and the *Army* way. And as long as you're in the Army, you're going to do it the *Army* way!"

Similarly, if you're going to be a success in life, you're going to have to do things God's way. The saying "United we stand; divided we fall" is more than a timeworn phrase. It is the key to our success. It is the key to taking the future.

The Challenge

Today, we stand at a crossroad. Our future is bright. The threshold is before us. Will we, having prepared ourselves and committed ourselves wholly to God, come together in unity and harmony to go out and take the future for God? It's up to each of us; the decision is ours to make.

We have a task in front of us—to do what God has called us to do. I am challenging you today to move up a notch and take the future for the Kingdom of God. And at the same time, you can take what I am saying and apply it to your natural life and your own future.

As a minister, I like to preach a message that not only will bind people together as a corporate body and propel us forward as the Church of the Lord Jesus Christ, but that will also help people individually. With preparation, commitment, and unity, we can accomplish anything. We can take the future!

Are you willing to make the commitment that it takes to be successful? Are you willing to take the baton, so to speak, and run for the finish line? Where your life is concerned, it's not up to me, your neighbor, your spouse, or anyone else. The decision is yours alone.

I challenge you today to move out of your comfort zone and become a success naturally and spiritually. God wants you to be a success here in this life. But let us also together become a success as the Church of the Lord Jesus Christ, because the world is full of questions and is waiting for an answer. And we have the Answer. Let's take Jesus to the world!

Chapter 2

Living in Success

Success without honor is an unseasoned dish;
it will satisfy your hunger, but it won't taste good.

Joe Paterno

The future is full of possibilities. You can make those possibilities realities by following God and walking out *His* plan for your life. You can control your destiny. Yesterday is gone, but tomorrow is new. Starting today, you have the opportunity to write success stories on the pages of your life's future. What will be written on the pages of your future will depend on you. Your future will be what *you* make it!

In Joshua chapter 3, we read about the Israelites preparing to cross the Jordan River.

JOSHUA 3:1–4 (NIV)

1   **Early in the morning Joshua and all the Israelites set out from Shittim and went to the Jordan, where they camped before crossing over.**

2   **After three days the officers went throughout the camp,**

3   **giving orders to the people: "When you see the ark of the covenant of the Lord your God, and the priests, who are Levites, carrying it, you are to move out from your positions and follow it.**

**4   Then you will know which way to go, since you have
never been this way before . . . ."**

In our text, we read that the Israelites had set out on a journey under God's direction and Joshua's command. Yet the
Israelites didn't even know where they were going. God told
them to follow the Ark of the Covenant. Then they would
know which way to go. They weren't supposed to get close to
the Ark; they were just supposed to follow it (v. 4). The Ark of
the Covenant represented the power and Presence of God. And
if the Israelites would follow the Presence of God, they would
reach their destiny and find success in Him.

Today we as Christians have the power and Presence of
God dwelling *inside* us (John 14:16–17). So when we don't
know which way to go, we should look to the Holy Spirit
inside us for direction. No matter what the world is saying or
what a particular situation looks like, we are to follow the leading of the Holy Spirit!

Many times, following God will seem irrational or illogical,
but God's ways are higher than our ways (Isa. 55:8–9). It might
look as though you're making the wrong decision or going the
wrong way, but if God said do it, it will turn out right.

It doesn't matter where you are or what circumstance
you're in—whether you live in a tent or a mansion, or whether
you have a penny or a million dollars—none of those things
can dominate you if you don't allow them to. If you are facing
adverse circumstances in life, you *can* change your circumstances and your destiny by simply following God and walking
out His plan for your life!

Someone might say, "Well, I *have* been walking with God
and obeying Him, but things don't seem to be changing." Your
situation might not change overnight. I personally know a
number of people who followed God and His leading for two
or three years even when it didn't look as though their situation was ever going to change. They refused to look at everything going on around them, because it would have been

impossible to follow God while looking at the circumstances. And they received the victory!

Remove the Hindrances

If you want to walk out God's plan for your life and take your future by storm, you need *to remove whatever it is that is hindering you* from walking with God in faith and obedience.

Many people continually struggle in certain areas, because they fail to remove their hindrance—the real source of their problem. For example, you wouldn't bail water out of a trough while the faucet is still on and water is flowing into the trough! But many people are "bailing out" of situations in their lives, yet they have never bothered to shut off the source of their problem. They're desperately fighting a never-ending battle— they're trying to stop the *effects* of the problem, yet never addressing the *cause* of the problem.

What I'm saying to you is that if you want to walk out God's plan for your life, you must *first* remove all the things that threaten to stall or stop your progress.

For example, one of the greatest hindrances to spiritual progress and to receiving from God is *the past*. Until you put your past behind you, you're going to be hindered from receiving God's best in the future. So don't focus on past mistakes and failures. Realize that if you have asked God for forgiveness, He is faithful and just to forgive you and to cleanse you from all unrighteousness (1 John 1:9). Believe that and walk on!

Forgiven and Forgotten

When God forgives, He forgets. Yet some Christians still say, "How can I expect to receive anything else from God, considering the kind of life I've led? I'm just lucky to be forgiven and in the family of God." But if you've been born again, it doesn't matter what kind of life you once led. Your past has been done away with, and you have been cleansed and made new by the shed blood of the Lord Jesus Christ!

Before you accepted Jesus as Savior, you might have always had to look over your shoulder, afraid that something from your past was going to catch up with you. But you don't have to look back anymore, because there's nothing there to catch up with you! Don't allow the devil to hinder you by bringing up memories from the past. Allowing yourself to be hindered by the past will cause you to miss God's blessings in the future. God has forgotten all your past mistakes and failures.

HEBREWS 10:16–17 (*NIV*)

16 "This is the covenant I will make with them after that time, says the Lord. I will put my laws in their hearts, and I will write them on their minds."

17 Then he adds: "Their sins and lawless acts I WILL REMEMBER NO MORE."

All the sins and lawless acts you ever committed were forgotten by God the moment you asked Him for forgiveness! So put aside the emotions and attitudes that come to you because of what happened in the past. The past doesn't exist anymore, so put it out of your mind. Renew your mind with the Word of God (Rom. 12:2).

Renewing your mind will change your emotional state. It can also help you restore broken relationships. If you are holding bad feelings in your heart because someone hurt you in the past, your attitude could be robbing you of fellowship with God and with others.

People who have been hurt by others tend to say, "I'll never trust anyone again." But just because they have been "burned" by someone in the past is no sign that everyone else will treat them the same way.

We must learn to let go of the past hurts, failures, and mistakes. We need to follow after peace with God and our fellow man and learn to fellowship with those of like faith.

Get Rid of Fear

Another hindrance that must be removed if you are going to walk out God's plan is *fear*. The Bible tells us that fear is not from God.

2 TIMOTHY 1:7
7   For God hath not given us the spirit of fear; but of power, and of love, and of a sound mind.

Many people become afraid when they don't know what is going to happen in the future. As Christians, we shouldn't fear facing the unknown. Didn't God say to the Israelites, in effect, "Follow Me, because you have never been this way before" (Joshua 3:3–4)? As we follow God, He will take care of us. We may not be able to see the future clearly, but we are walking with the One who can!

The enemy constantly tries to make us afraid. He'll say, "All right, the Lord has provided for you in the past, but what about now? How is He going to provide for you in this situation?" When the devil or anyone else asks us that question we should say, "I don't know, but God *does!*"

The devil will try to hinder you with fear. But you've got to learn to get rid of that hindrance by reading and meditating on the Word of God and then walking out the Word in faith!

God has been calming man's fears throughout time, since the beginning of Creation. And God is still telling man today, "Don't be afraid. The written Word is with you. The Living Word also abides in you. And greater is He that is *in* you than he that is in the world" (1 John 4:4)! God will always be greater than the devil! You need to remember that when you face challenges as you're walking out God's plan for your life.

Charting Your Course

To become the success God wants you to be, you must first remove any hindrance the enemy uses to try to keep you from receiving what God has for you, including fear and thoughts of the past. The second thing you must do if you want to experience God's best is *to chart your course according to God's plan.* After you discover God's plan for your life, you should begin to set your goals in line with it.

By way of illustration, a pilot's job is to fly a plane. But he doesn't just say, "I'm going to fly to Dallas," and then get in an airplane and take off. No! Before he ever gets on the plane, he has to study maps and chart his course. Then he files his flight plan with the proper authorities who can either grant or refuse him permission to make the flight.

But that's not all a pilot has to do. After he has laid out a course, he still has to check the weather. It may be beautiful where he is, but in the direction he is headed, there could be some weather conditions that he needs to avoid. If that's the case, the pilot needs to redirect his course. He shouldn't just say, "Well, I already filed my flight plan; I'm going to follow my plan anyway!" If he starts flying and runs into some stiff crosswinds or another situation he isn't prepared to handle, it could take him miles off course.

A pilot relies on his instruments to help him stay on his charted course. One such instrument, called an altimeter, measures altitude. If a pilot doesn't continually check his altimeter as he is flying, he could end up flying right into the ground! The altimeter provides information that tells the pilot how to change his course while he is in flight. If the pilot ignores these warnings and then crashes the plane, the accident would be the result of "pilot error."

When it comes to spiritual things, a lot of people experience "pilot error," because they ignore the warning signals the Holy Spirit is sending them. They need to realize that as they walk with God, they must continually be sensitive to the Holy Spirit and make adjustments in their lives; otherwise they're going to get into trouble. Following the Lord's leading and charting your course is an important part of the divine strategy that will put you over in life when others are falling by the wayside.

Planning a Strategy

Even the world recognizes the importance of planning a strategy. In business, the presidents of corporations sit around conference tables planning for the future of their companies. In athletics, coaches also plan their strategies to win games. Thinking and planning ahead is of vital importance.

Some Christians think that after they get born again and filled with the Holy Spirit, they don't have to use their intellects anymore. But we're supposed to gather information, think rationally, and then put together and carry out a plan that will make us successful—spiritually and naturally.

Actually, you're not going to be successful naturally until you're successful spiritually. You could be rich and possess every material thing you want—houses, lands, cars, and so forth—and the world will call you successful. But unless you're born again, you really have nothing (Mark 8:36)! Yet you could be born again and be living below your rights and privileges in Christ, just barely getting by. That's not good, either. Jesus came that we might have abundant, successful, victorious life (John 10:10)! The Bible is the "guide book" by which we can formulate a plan to follow God all the way to success!

Too many people are satisfied with second best. As believers, the only time we should be fully satisfied is when we walk through the "pearly gates" and enter our heavenly home! Until then, the Word of God says we are to strive for maturity. We cannot strive for maturity and at the same time be totally satisfied with where we are.

I'm not saying you shouldn't enjoy life where you are today and that you should always be dissatisfied even when you are experiencing God's blessings. I'm saying you should be thankful for what God has done for you, but be dissatisfied because you know that the Bible says there is more (Eph. 3:20)!

Every time you receive a benefit from God, enjoy it and give thanks for it, but realize that more awaits you. Then lay out your plan to go after it according to the Word.

Lay Hold of God's Strength

After you've removed the things that could hinder you and you've charted your course, the final thing you need to do is *to lay hold of the strength and power you need for success.*

Many people fall short of achieving success because they rely on their own strength. But the believer's strength, power, and ability come from God.

PHILIPPIANS 4:13

13 I can do all things THROUGH CHRIST which strengtheneth me.

We can do all things through Christ who strengthens us. *All* things! That means we can accomplish whatever we set out to do because God is giving us the strength to do it. We have the inner strength we need because Jesus Christ is our power source! We don't serve God in our own power or might. We serve God by the strength of the Holy Spirit within us.

This truth was illustrated when a remnant of Jews led by Zerubbabel began to rebuild the temple of the Lord which had been destroyed earlier by the Babylonians. Their enemies repeatedly tried to stop them, but God assured the Israelites that the temple would be completely restored because the Holy Spirit would strengthen them to do the work.

ZECHARIAH 4:6

6 Then he answered and spake unto me, saying, This is the word of the Lord unto Zerubbabel, saying, NOT BY MIGHT, NOR BY POWER, BUT BY MY SPIRIT, SAITH THE LORD OF HOSTS.

Our strength, power, and ability will produce nothing unless we are infused with power from on High—power from the Holy Spirit (2 Cor. 10:4). I'm not saying that we shouldn't use the talents and abilities God has given us. I'm saying that unless our abilities are infused with the power of Him Who has redeemed us, they are really useless.

Friend, the future lies before you spotless and bright. The pages of your future history are blank. Start right now to remove the things that may have hindered you in the past. Begin charting a new course to receive success with God. Then tap into God's strength and power and walk out His plan for your life. No matter what the circumstances, at the end of each day, may you be able to write by faith, "I have been a success today because of God!"

Chapter 3

Tomorrow Begins Today

The future is purchased by the present.

Samuel Johnson

⊷ ⊷ ⧏✦⧐ ⊶ ⊶

Your future is not off in the distance somewhere. What you do today affects your tomorrow. So we could say that tomorrow—your future—starts right now.

We learn from the Bible that God always has His children do something *today* to prepare them for *tomorrow*.

JOSHUA 3:5

5 And Joshua said unto the people, Sanctify yourselves: for TO MORROW the Lord will do wonders among you.

Joshua made this statement the day before the Israelites were to cross the Jordan River into Canaan. According to Joshua's command, the Israelites were to sanctify themselves. In other words, they were to become ceremonially clean. There were things they had to do in the natural before they were considered ready to travel.

We don't have to become ceremonially clean, because we are made clean through Jesus Christ. So for us, this verse simply means that there are things we must do to be ready for what tomorrow, the future, holds.

Now I want to read Joshua 3:5 from the *New International Version*.

JOSHUA 3:5 (*NIV*)
5   Joshua told the people, "Consecrate yourselves, for tomorrow the Lord will do amazing things among you."

In this modern age, we understand the word "consecrate" better than we understand the word "sanctify." To the Israelites, the word "sanctify" or "consecrate" meant going through certain acts of purification. It meant getting themselves physically pure in order to be able to move with God.

For us as Christians, consecration means to set ourselves apart from the world and be sold out to God in every area of our lives.

Where Are You Headed?

What do I mean when I say that tomorrow begins today? First, let's study the word "tomorrow" and find out what it means. The prefix "to" means *movement toward.* And the word "morrow" means *the future* or *the day which is to follow the present.* Understanding those definitions, we can understand the phrase "tomorrow begins today" to mean that our direction at this present moment should be toward the future.

You see, tomorrow starts today in the sense that if you don't take care of what needs to be done today, you will not be ready for tomorrow. And if you aren't prepared for tomorrow, you could miss out when tomorrow becomes today.

Again, in Joshua 3:5, Joshua said unto the Israelites, "Sanctify [or consecrate] yourselves for tomorrow. . . ." Joshua was telling them to get ready today for something that was going to happen tomorrow. If you study the Old Testament, you will find that many times before the children of Israel were able to be involved in certain feasts or sacrifices, they had to satisfy the Law's ceremonial rites and cleansings.

Remember, the Israelites weren't filled with the Holy Spirit. They weren't even born of the Spirit. The Father, Son, and Holy Spirit did not tabernacle in them. In fact, most Israelites weren't in contact with God at all. The only people who were in contact with God were the prophet, priest, and king. They were in contact with Him because they were the ones who were anointed.

God is so pure and holy that whenever He was going to move, He told Israel ahead of time so they could prepare themselves and be clean. If they did not prepare themselves, they would not be able to go where God was moving.

Don't Be Left Behind

In the natural, when you prepare for a road trip, you know that you have to start preparing long before it's time to actually begin the trip. If you are going to take a bus, for example, and the bus is scheduled to leave the next morning at five o'clock, it would be wise to get everything ready the night before so you don't miss the bus.

But suppose you don't get everything ready the night before and then wake up late the next morning. You'll be trying to get everything ready in a hurry, and by the time you arrive to catch the bus, it could be gone.

Something similar actually happened to some of my church members one time when they were planning to go with the church on a trip somewhere. When they were left behind, they called the church office and said, "Pastor, the bus drove off and left us!"

I asked them, "What time was the bus supposed to leave?"

They said, "Well, it was supposed to leave at five o'clock this morning."

I asked, "What time did you get there?"

"5:15."

Now what did the people who were left behind expect? The bus left when it was supposed to; they just weren't ready on time!

If those people had taken care of everything the day before, they would have been ready for "tomorrow" and on time for their departure.

Tomorrow actually begins today! In other words, your success tomorrow depends on your actions today.

Follow the Guide

I want us to learn some things from the pattern that the Israelites followed. The Ark of the Covenant went before the Israelites as they traveled. The Ark of the Covenant represented the Presence of God. In the dispensation or age in which we live, we have the Holy Spirit to guide us and direct us. Israel as a nation was to follow the Ark of the Covenant wherever it went. If the Ark went straight and then turned left, the Israelites were supposed to turn left. They weren't supposed to keep going straight.

Every time the Ark of the Covenant stopped, the children of Israel stopped. When the Ark moved, they moved. They followed the Ark because the power of God went wherever the Ark did. And the Israelites wanted to follow the power of God.

The Ark of the Covenant was the Israelites' guide and the indicator whereby they knew when and where to travel. If Israel didn't follow the Ark of the Covenant, they removed themselves from the protection of God. The protection of God is where His Presence is.

Now we have the anointing or Guide—the Holy Spirit—within us. One thing that causes problems for many Christians today is not following the Holy Spirit. They may follow the Holy Spirit for a while, but then He turns, so to speak, and goes a different direction, and they're still going down the same road they were on.

Many of us have found ourselves in that position at one time or another. We need to be sure to follow the Holy Spirit as He leads us on the path God has prepared for us.

Consecrate Yourself to God

The Ark of the Covenant was not something to be treated or handled lightly. Before the reign of King David, priest Eli's sons, Phineas and Hophni, apparently fouled things up for Israel by bringing the Ark down to the battlefield (Num. 4:15; 1 Sam. 4). The Philistines captured the sacred Ark and won the battle.

Unfortunately for the Philistines, they didn't know the Ark of the Covenant was sacred and holy. As the story goes, they ended up trying to give the Ark back to Israel (1 Sam. 6:2). As the Ark moved from place to place, different ones would cry out, saying in effect, "Hey! Take this thing. It's causing us all kinds of problems" (see 1 Sam. 4–6 and 2 Sam. 6). And eventually, the Ark wound up at the house of an Israelite named Obed-Edom (2 Sam. 6:10–11).

Obed-Edom understood the importance of the Ark, and he ceremonially cleansed himself every time he had to go near it. Because of his consecration, his household was immensely blessed. When you have the anointing or the power of God with you, you're going to be blessed. But it's important that you learn how to treat the anointing. Of course, that's another subject entirely, but I think that point needs to be mentioned here.

When King David went to return the Ark to Jerusalem, he didn't handle the Ark according to God's orders and messed everything up (1 Chron. 13). David meant well, but he didn't do what God said to do concerning the Ark of the Covenant.

That's one thing that is the matter with many Christians today. They mean well, but they're not doing things God's way. As I said before, if you want to be blessed, you're going to have to do things God's way.

When you aren't completely consecrated to God, you start getting off track a little bit here and a little bit there, doing a few things that you shouldn't be doing. But then you start having problems in a lot of areas. Why? Because you aren't following

God's plan for your life. When you aren't following God, you don't have His power in your life because His power or anointing can't be involved where there is any kind of sin.

Success in Your Personal Life

Tomorrow begins today first in our personal lives. Who I am today will determine who I am tomorrow. What I do today will determine where I'm able to go tomorrow. What I think and say today will determine my attitude for tomorrow.

Often what happens to you tomorrow depends on what you do today. Many people say, "I'm just living day by day." But when we live day by day, we're not thinking about tomorrow; therefore, we're not preparing ourselves for tomorrow.

Someone might say that preparing for tomorrow keeps us from looking for Jesus' return. No, it doesn't. According to the Bible, we are to "occupy" until Jesus returns (Luke 19:13). The word "occupy" implies that we are to be involved with successfully living here on earth. Yes, we are to look forward to Jesus' return, but in the meantime, we are to be concerned about what's going on down here.

Many Christians are floating around, so to speak, without any focus or goal in life. These people are saved and baptized with the Holy Ghost, but they're "over here" one day and "over there" the next. They aren't stable or focused. Because they have no focus in their life, many times they're a spiritual accident looking for a place to happen!

When you have a focus in your life—when you know where you're going and what you're going to do—then you start preparing for tomorrow *today*. Unfortunately, many people end up in trouble because they never prepare for tomorrow by building up their faith today. Everything in their life may be fine. Everything's hunky-dory, and there are no problems. So these people don't continue to study the Word, and they don't continue to keep their faith built up. What happens? When tomorrow arrives, the devil is able to knock them upside the head, so to speak, because they aren't ready. People who don't prepare today won't be ready for tomorrow.

Take Your Vitamins!

This principle of preparing for tomorrow can be illustrated using a very natural example—vitamins. There are certain things I do every morning, such as taking my vitamins, that aren't necessarily to help my body on that particular day. I do them so that my physical body will be all right tomorrow—and the next day and the next.

I have several kinds of vitamins—vitamin A, C, E, and so forth—and I take one of each every morning. I take them because medical experts have told me that it is a wise thing to do in order to supplement the regular vitamins and minerals found in the various foods I eat. If you do any reading at all about the health of people in America, you'll discover that Americans in general don't get enough of those particular vitamins because our eating habits have become less than desirable.

And because our bodies don't store vitamin C, we have to take vitamin C every day. If we don't, we're not preparing for tomorrow. Now it's possible to acquire too much vitamin A, but most people consume enough of it. But I'm not just taking vitamins to benefit me today. In fact, except the vitamin C, the vitamins I took today won't do me that much good *today*. But they will benefit me tomorrow—in the future.

We know this principle to be true in certain areas in our lives, such as in our finances and in dealing with our physique. We understand that what we do today in the natural realm affects our tomorrow, but we don't apply that same principle to the spiritual realm. We need to understand that what we do today will also determine our spiritual condition tomorrow.

We can't afford to live loosely today. In other words, we can't tell off-colored jokes and run with the wrong crowd today and expect to be spiritually strong tomorrow. We can't forsake assembling together with others of like faith today and expect to be strong tomorrow.

It's not enough to just go to church and expect to be spiritually strong. You have to go to church with people of like precious faith. If you go to a church where they don't believe in line with the Bible the way you do, it will be like short-circuiting a battery, only you will be short-circuiting your spirit. It will drain the power of God out of you to assemble together continually with those who peddle doubt and unbelief.

A born-again, Spirit-filled Christian shouldn't pal around with people who are in the world. Now I realize you have to work with them and associate with them on that basis. But I'm talking about being buddies with and always hanging out with non-Christians, doing the things they do and going where they go.

You can't pal around with those who are serving the world without it affecting your spiritual life. What we do today will determine our tomorrows.

Built to Last

Think of your future as a building that you are daily endeavoring to construct. A building made with inferior materials will not stand for very long. You can build a building that looks good on the surface, but if the foundation or foundational material is inferior, the building will soon crumble.

We bought the first building on the RHEMA campus from a man who installed drywall for a living. He ran out of funds before he finished building, so in the soffits around the building, he put regular Sheetrock instead of the proper waterproof Sheetrock that he was supposed to use. Then he just put stucco on top of the regular Sheetrock.

When we first bought the building, we didn't know what we were in for. We had to install new carpet and do a lot of other things to get ready for the first day of classes at RHEMA Bible Training Center. It wasn't very long after we began these improvements that the walls began to literally crumble! I couldn't figure out what in the world was going on. I had the building examined and learned that the stucco was falling apart. Not only that, but I learned then that the Sheetrock under the stucco wasn't the proper waterproof kind that should have been used in the first place.

When Sheetrock gets wet, it absorbs the water and begins to crumble. If the Sheetrock is part of the ceiling, eventually the whole thing will collapse. The building looked good as far as the eye could see, but it was deteriorating from the inside out!

If you have ever built a house or any kind of structure, you know that you must build in such a way to ensure that the structure will stand long after you build it. You make sure that the concrete is the consistency it's supposed to be as you pour the foundation.

You even run tests on the foundation for a certain number of days. And a certain number of days after the cement has been poured, you check it again and again until it is what is called "cured." That means the cement has dried completely and that it will withstand the elements and hold the weight that it's to hold.

If you use inferior concrete when working with driveways and such, the concrete will begin to crack, crumble, and break apart long before it should. If you pour concrete when it's the wrong temperature outside and you don't do certain things such as add certain chemicals to the mixture, your foundation won't last. It won't be there tomorrow, so to speak.

If you build a house with inferior lumber or other inferior products, after about six months the house will start falling apart. It may have looked good to start with. There are a lot of houses that look really good on the outside, but aren't built properly on the inside where it counts. Also, a good exterior may hide what is within the walls and the wood, such as termites.

I remember hearing a story about a family who bought a particular house. One day the teenage boys were wrestling, and they threw one another into the wall. When they hit the wall, the whole house started falling down around them. The wall they hit happened to be a supporting wall, and half the house fell down!

The studs had been eaten out from the inside by termites, so although the house appeared to be secure, it was just barely standing.

There are a lot of people today who talk the right talk and even act right before others, but they're not right on the inside. On the other hand, there are some people who may not look "just right" on the outside who have committed themselves to being right on the inside. For those people, it won't be very long until the good that is on the inside will be manifested externally. The person who seemingly is perfect but has bitterness and hatred on the inside will also eventually have what's on the inside work its way to the outside.

We are not building a structure of stone or wood. We are building a life. And a life built upon wrong ideas and wrong principles will not stand the test of time. But a life that is built upon the principles and values of the Word of God will be here tomorrow, the next day, and the day after that. This kind of life will stand secure throughout all your tomorrows because it was built properly upon the proper foundation.

Many people are saying, "Oh, if I can just make it by until tomorrow, my problems will all be over." No, they won't. If you don't do anything today about your problems, they will still be with you tomorrow. If you want to change your tomorrows, then change your todays. Your tomorrow begins today.

Consecration as the Key to Success

We saw from our text in Joshua chapter 3 that Joshua's first plea to the people was for them to consecrate themselves. Consecration is the first step toward a successful tomorrow. What does consecration mean to us today? It means that we set ourselves apart from the world's system and way of doing things. If we're true believers, then let's act like it—in the way we live, talk, and dress.

It's real easy to consecrate or commit yourself to something when life is going great. It's another thing to be consecrated when everything is going wrong and it looks as though you're going backward instead of forward. But if we want a successful future, we must be consecrated to God and His Word in the face of any obstacle that comes along.

To be "consecrated" means to be submitted and devoted to God. The only time God will be able to use you is when you're truly submitted to Him. As we say in Texas, you must be submitted—*lock, stock, and barrel.* That means you are submitted wholly and completely.

If we're going to consecrate ourselves to God, we've got to get rid of excess baggage. Some things in our life may not be wrong in that they may not be sin, per se, but they are excess baggage in that they weigh us down and keep us from being sold out to God and doing what He wants us to do.

Removing Excess Baggage

Many times when I was in training as a soldier in the United States Army, I had to march with a pack of various supplies on my back. But when soldiers get out on the battlefield and are in the heat of the battle, they don't have a pack on their back. They may wear an ammunition bandoleer, and they may have a canteen and first aid kit on their belt, but they get rid of anything that isn't absolutely necessary in a battle situation.

You don't need a change of clothes and a tent when you're in the midst of battle. Those things aren't necessarily bad to carry, but at the wrong time, they will weigh you down and keep you from accomplishing your objective. In war, you need to get rid of everything except the bare essentials.

I remember when I was in training and doing hill assaults. My training group marched out there with all of our paraphernalia on our backs, but when we got ready to simulate battle conditions taking the hill, we got rid of everything we could. Why? Because we didn't want anything slowing us down.

When we were making a run from one log on the ground to another, we wanted to move as fast as possible! The point of the exercise was to learn to outrun and dodge enemy fire! We had to crawl underneath barbwire while real bullets were flying over our heads. When it came time for me to move out, I got down as low as I could and took off as hard as I could to the next piece of cover I could find.

When we were running the infiltration course underneath barbwire, dodging bullets and so forth, we carried our ammunition and our weapon, but we didn't carry those packs around with us!

Unfortunately, there are some Christians who are trying to win spiritual battles while they are weighed down and hindered by all kinds of excess baggage.

When I ran track, I used to train by wearing weights on my legs, baseball cleats, and sweats while I ran practice heats. But when I got ready to run in the race, I took off the weights, the baseball cleats, and sweats.

The baseball cleats probably weighed four pounds. During the race, I wore track shoes, which probably weighed a few ounces. I took off the sweatsuit, which would only get heavier the more I ran and perspired. I wore a pair of running shorts and a singlet top to race in. I got rid of anything that would impair me or slow me down.

You can't run successfully or win battles carrying excess baggage. The same is true in the spiritual arena. We've got to get rid of baggage that will hold us back and weigh us down.

Judging Ourselves

Some Christians do not like to hear or talk about the word "judgment." But, friend, in the Bible there is as much written about judgment as there is about other subjects people like to hear messages on, such as faith and prosperity. And the Bible tells us that if we don't judge ourselves, eventually, we will bring God's judgment upon us (1 Cor. 11:31–32).

A common problem among Christians today is they are not receiving a well-balanced spiritual diet. In the natural, people talk about eating well-balanced, healthy meals. Parents do their best when their children are young and at home to see that they eat well-balanced meals from the basic food groups—proteins, grains, vegetables, fruit, and dairy. But parents may not be able to monitor as much what their children eat when the kids are older and at school or out with friends.

Children may not always like to eat fruits or vegetables. But we can't just eat sweets all the time and expect to have a healthy physical body. Neither can we just eat meat all the time. There is not just one single food group that contains all the vitamins and minerals that a body needs to be healthy.

The basic food groups are the main things taught in nutrition class in school. It is common knowledge that if a person does not eat properly, his or her body (metabolism, immune system, and so forth) will be out of balance and unhealthy.

Many times, people who have mistreated their body will get in a healing line and want hands laid on them in prayer. After talking to them, I learn that they don't need healing, per se; they just need to eat properly and rest properly, and their body will come back in line.

Some Christians mistreat their spiritual man in much the same way a person mistreats his natural man. These Christians don't feed on all of the Word. They just like the "sweets." They have itching ears, so to speak, and will only listen to the kind of teaching they want to hear. Sometimes they don't even care whether or not the teaching is sound doctrinally. As long as the message is what they want to hear, they can leave the service feeling good.

It seems as though many people today don't want to hear or say anything about the blood of Jesus, right and wrong, or Heaven and hell. No one says anything about judgment anymore. But we must learn to judge ourselves—to determine the life we must live today in order to live the life God has destined us to live tomorrow.

Guilty by Association

Everyone is quick to judge sexual sin and murder as wrong, yet when you study the Word of God you find that God is, at least, equally opposed to such sins as lying and deceit.

Some people who are self-employed are cheating the government by operating on a cash basis when they sell goods or perform services. They say, "Pay me in cash. I don't want any records of this transaction." I don't like to do business with that kind of person. I don't want to be party to wrongdoing. Sometimes when dealing with contractors, you don't know they operate that way until you're already doing business with them. In that case, just pay them what you owe them and let them go on down the road.

So many times a person may not be doing anything wrong himself, but he can be party to someone else's wrongdoing and that makes him guilty by association. As far as the law is concerned, he might as well have done the deed himself.

Someone who cheats on his income taxes may argue, "Well, I don't like the tax structure in this country."

But when it comes to paying taxes, the Bible says to "render unto Caesar what is Caesar's" (Luke 20:25). If you study history, you'll learn that Caesar wasn't always right in everything he did. Yet Jesus told the disciples to give to Caesar what was his. In other words, Jesus was saying that if we do what's right on the natural side of things, He will take care of us.

Success in Your Home

We've seen how tomorrow begins today in your personal life. Now let's study how tomorrow begins today in your home. Relationships with your spouse, your children, your brothers and sisters begin today–not tomorrow. For example, is the love that should exist between husband and wife operating in your home?

Someone might say, "We're going to start working on our relationship tomorrow. We're going to start walking in love tomorrow." With that attitude, you will never start. Tomorrow will turn into today, and then before you know it, it will be yesterday.

You have to start building today what you want to see standing tomorrow. We all know people who have been saying for years, "I'm going to start an exercise program tomorrow" or "I'm going on a diet tomorrow."

I remember a time when I had been saying that I was going to lose some weight and start an exercise program. At one point, I finally said, "Tomorrow begins *today*," and I started exercising. I lost twelve pounds in the first three weeks.

I kept putting off until tomorrow what needed to be done today. If I would have kept doing that, I would have never started exercising and never would have lost weight. And I'd still be saying, "I'm going to start exercising. I'll do it *tomorrow*."

Parents, we need to be raising our families in the nurture and admonition of the Lord (Eph. 6:4). Are you as a parent disciplining your children in line with the Word of God? You discipline today for tomorrow's results.

Are you leading your home correctly by teaching and by example? Tomorrow begins today in your house too. What your small child will be when he or she becomes a teenager and adult depends on what you teach and live before him or her today.

Success in Your Church

Tomorrow begins today in your own life, in your home, and in your local church. I have already talked about what this means in your personal life and in your home. Now I want to look at how this applies in the local church.

The strength of your local church depends upon the strength of the spiritual life of its members. You've heard the saying that a chain is only as strong as its weakest link.

The rest of that chain may be strong enough to pull a 70,000-pound truck. But if only one link, for some reason or another, has lost its ability to pull that much weight, the chain will break at that weak link, rendering the whole chain useless. In much the same way, each Christian is a part of a local body of believers and a part of the Body of Christ as a whole. Each Christian must do his part to stay spiritually strong to help pull his share of the weight in service to the Lord. Both the local body and the entire Body are only as strong spiritually as the weakest individual.

That's one reason we should be concerned about one another. For example, what do you do if two or three services go by and you don't see a particular person or family at church? Do you bother to check on them or ask someone else about them, or do you just let them go their way? The pastoral staff can't keep up with everyone. But you as a local church member can check on some of these people. Sometimes all they need is someone to give them an encouraging word and say, "Hey, I noticed you haven't been at church. Can I help you in any way? Can I pray with you? Do you need a ride?" We as a church must be concerned about holding on to the people we have and helping them stay strong spiritually.

There are many people who are doing what I call "hitchhiking" at church. In other words, they don't support the church financially, but they enjoy the benefits that result from others supporting the church financially. These "hitchhikers" reap what others have sown. They never get involved in supporting the local church. They only want to benefit from the church.

On the other hand, when visitors come to RHEMA Bible Church and see all of the outreaches we have, they get to reap what other people have sown over a period of time. Then when *they* get involved and start sowing, new people who come in after them will reap benefits from *their* giving. That is perfectly fine, and the way it ought to be. The problem starts when too many people just continue to hitchhike. They're riding on someone else's tithing and giving.

In the natural, a person can only hitchhike so far before the driver stops the car, opens the door, and says, "This is as far as you're going." It works the same way with God; a person can only "hitchhike" so far before God requires that he contribute to His work.

We should care about the future as it relates to the local church just as much as we care about our own tomorrows. But many people live for what they can have today and give no thought for tomorrow. And they have the same attitude toward the church. I've heard it taught in church, "Don't give any thought for tomorrow. Just live for today." If you don't live your life today with tomorrow in mind, there might not be any tomorrow—no future. We should care about tomorrow because tomorrow is a word that has hope in it. We sacrifice, we work, we pray, we give to the church today so it will be here for our family and for others tomorrow.

Tomorrow begins today. Tomorrow begins today in our personal Christian lives. And our homes of tomorrow depend upon our home of today. Our church of tomorrow will be what we are making it today. Remember, we must consecrate ourselves today for what the Lord will do tomorrow.

Tomorrow begins today. Get hold of that thought, and begin to do something about your tomorrow—*today*.

Chapter 4

What Are You Looking At?

Have plenty of courage.
God is stronger than the devil.
We are on the winning side.

John Chapman

As you face the future, situations and circumstances in life may appear overwhelming. But that's only in the natural. If you will open your spiritual eyes, you will clearly see that God and all of Heaven are on your side!

In Second Kings chapter 6, we read that Elisha's servant Gehazi went outside one morning and saw the entire city surrounded by the Syrian army.

2 KINGS 6:14–15

14 [The king of Syria sent] **. . . thither horses, and chariots, and a great host: and they came by night, and compassed the city about.**

15 **And when** [Gehazi] **the servant of the man of God was risen early, and gone forth, behold, an host compassed the city both with horses and chariots. And his servant said unto him, Alas, my master! how shall we do?**

Gehazi focused on what was going on in the natural, and he became panic-stricken. He had a *fleshly* or natural outlook. But there is another outlook: the *spiritual* or supernatural outlook.

I want to ask you a question. When you're facing a test or trial, what are you looking at? Your outlook will determine your attitude—whether you're up or down—and your attitude will determine your outcome—whether you do or don't receive all that God has for you.

Gehazi was looking at what he could see in the natural, so he became frightened. But Elisha told him, "Fear not!"

2 KINGS 6:16–17

16 And he [Elisha] **answered, Fear not: for they that be with us are more than they that be with them.**

17 And Elisha prayed, and said, Lord, I pray thee, open his eyes, that he may see. And the Lord opened the eyes of the young man; and he saw: and, behold, the mountain was full of horses and chariots of fire round about Elisha.

Elisha had a spiritual outlook. His spiritual outlook took notice that the army of God was close by—unseen, unheard, and undetected in the natural, but more powerful than the natural Syrian army.

The outlook you have will determine whether you are operating in a spirit of fear or a spirit of power. The *natural* outlook will cause you to operate in a spirit of *fear*. But the *supernatural* outlook will cause you to operate in a spirit of *power*.

2 TIMOTHY 1:7

7 For God hath not given us the spirit of FEAR; but of POWER, and of love, and of a sound mind.

God has not given us the spirit of *fear*, but the spirit of *power*! This verse is talking about spirits—in particular, the spirit of fear and the spirit of power. And, thank God, we have the spirit of power!

If you continue to look at your situation in the natural, you will undoubtedly yield to the spirit of fear. That can cause feelings of panic, unworthiness, inadequacy, despair, or depression to control and influence you. But when you look at your situation in the *super*natural, you will yield to the spirit of power, the spirit of love, the spirit of a sound mind!

Let's look at the last clause of Second Timothy 1:7 which talks about a sound mind. God has given us the spirit of a sound mind—not a spirit of confusion! If you were to talk to many people today, you would find that they are confused. They don't know who they are or where they're going in life. They're in a panic because of the spirit of fear. They're afraid because they don't know what's going to happen tomorrow.

Friend, I want to tell you something. I'm not confused. I know who I am in Christ, and I know where I'm going. I even know what's going to happen tomorrow. Someone might ask, "How do you know what's going to happen tomorrow?" I know what's going to happen because I know what the Bible says! The Bible says God always causes us to triumph in Christ (2 Cor. 2:14)!

It's up to you to decide whether you're going to operate in the natural or the supernatural, in the flesh or in the spirit, in fear or in power.

The Truth Will Set You Free

Elisha's servant focused on those who were arrayed against him. Similarly, too many Christians are always looking at what the devil is doing or talking about what the devil said.

Who cares what the devil said? He's a liar; he couldn't tell the truth if he wanted to! The devil doesn't know everything—he just thinks he does. Even in the natural, we don't want to listen to someone talk about what they *think* they know.

For example, in a court of law, a person's opinion or what he or she *thinks* doesn't mean a thing. As a witness, if someone starts giving his opinion, the opposing attorney would probably object. And, most of the time, the judge will rule that what the witness said is not admissible as evidence. Why? Because they only want to hear what people *know*.

Well, God *knows* what He's talking about! John 8:32 says, *"And ye shall know the truth, and the truth shall make you free."* The truth—not what some preacher said, not what someone thinks or believes—will make you free. Knowing the truth will give you power!

Look Beyond the Natural

I admit that it's easy to get into the flesh or the natural when you see all the things that are happening in our world today. Often, the world is not a very pretty place. There are all kinds of things coming against us as believers, because the devil is trying to destroy us.

But when you begin to focus on the natural things coming against you, you're headed for defeat. You cannot concentrate on the natural and stay in faith. You have to get out of the natural and into the supernatural. You must have eyes that look beyond what you can see just in the natural. Second Corinthians 4:18 makes that clear.

2 CORINTHIANS 4:18

18 While WE LOOK NOT AT THE THINGS WHICH ARE SEEN, BUT AT THE THINGS WHICH ARE NOT SEEN: for the things which are seen are TEMPORAL; but the things which are not seen are eternal.

That's right in line with what we read in Second Kings 6:16 and 17. We know that what Elisha's servant Gehazi saw in the natural was temporal or temporary, because, according to Second Corinthians 4:18, *". . . the things which are seen are temporal; but the things which are not seen are eternal."* When Gehazi was able to see into the supernatural realm, he saw the powerful army of God that was going to defeat the enemy.

It's the things you *can't* see that are often the most important. The things you can't see—the eternal things of the Spirit—are permanent. For example, you can't see God, but He's omnipresent—everywhere at all times. He can't be seen, but He's there with you.

Looking only at the seen will defeat you, but looking at the unseen will bring you victory and cause you to say about your situation what God says about it. Romans 4:17 says that God calls those things that be not as though they were.

ROMANS 4:17

17 (As it is written, I have made thee a father of many nations,) before him whom he believed, even God, who quickeneth the dead, AND CALLETH THOSE THINGS WHICH BE NOT AS THOUGH THEY WERE.

As you refuse to look at the natural and begin to focus only on the supernatural, you, too, can begin calling those things that be not as though they were!

How do you "call those things that be not as though they were"? Well, when you don't see healing, you can begin to call your body healed. Whether or not you can see your healing, it exists. You probably won't see it at first, but it exists nevertheless. And pretty soon, it will manifest in the natural, and you will see it with your own eyes.

The Eye of Faith

What are you looking at? Are you looking only at the natural things around you as Elisha's servant did? Or are you looking with the eye of faith as the prophet Elisha did? When you look with the eye of faith, you see things differently. You see healing and health when the circumstances are saying sickness and disease. You see prosperity when the circumstances say poverty and lack. You see victory when the circumstances say defeat.

When we built the RHEMA Bible Church auditorium, some people said, "It can't be done. Nothing like this has ever been built." In fact, the metal building company we contracted had to buy new computer software to do all the engineering computations.

I would go out to the building site when there was nothing but a pile of dirt out there. Sometimes I would take the pastoral staff with me. I would stand there, gesture, and say to them, "Here's the pulpit. The pews start over here and go all the way up. The balcony is up there, and the choir and orchestra are right here. Can't you just see it?"

At first, they all said, "No." But, thank God, after a little while, they began to grab hold of the vision. I could "see" what wasn't there in the natural.

That's what you're going to have to do in your own life. When the devil tells you that something you're believing God for is not going to happen, you're going to have to see it happening—not with eyes of the flesh, but with the eyes of your spirit.

I refused to get in the flesh and in fear when people asked me, "How are you going to pay for that building?" I answered, "In the natural, I don't know. But I'm looking at what I can't see. I know that God told me that this building would be the easiest building that's ever been paid for on this campus." And today I can testify that it was!

Your Outlook Determines Your Outcome

What you're looking at will lead you to victory or defeat. You have to begin to look at the unseen and call those things that be not as though they were (Rom. 4:17). Even though you can't see it, you still have to begin to say by faith, "I can see it."

Begin to see good things taking place in your life. The devil may have had you down for a long time. He may have been telling you that your dreams are never going to come true, and it may look as if they're not. But what does the devil know? He's a liar. Look beyond the natural and see what you're believing for as already done! Then begin to call it done!

You have to come to the realization that there are really only two outlooks: the fleshly, or natural, outlook and the spiritual, or supernatural, outlook. Then make up your mind about which outlook you're going to have! As I said previously, your outlook will determine your outcome. It's not necessarily how much you pray. In other words, your prayer life doesn't always determine your outcome. I'm not minimizing prayer in the least. I believe in prayer. But you can pray and then begin to focus on and talk about the wrong things, and your praying will be in vain.

If you're looking at your circumstances with just your natural eyes, you're going to find yourself wringing your hands and saying, "What am I going to do now?" But when you're looking with your spiritual eyes, as Elisha's servant finally did, you will see that "they that be with you are more than they that be with them" (2 Kings 6:16). God has already taken care of the situation for you!

Set your eyes on the supernatural and begin acting in line with God's Word! See your success and victory with the eye of the spirit!

Chapter 5

What Kind of Attitude Do You Have?

Ability is what you're capable of doing.

Motivation determines what you do.

Attitude determines how well you do it.

Lou Holtz

———— ≖✦≖ ————

As I said in the previous chapter, your outlook determines your outcome. This is not only true concerning what you're looking at, but it is also true concerning what kind of attitude you have. Whether or not you take the future by storm depends on several things—one of them is your attitude.

We've all heard people say, "So-and-so has an attitude!" Or, "So-and-so copped an attitude with me." Sometimes, we have to ignore the attitude of others, grit our teeth, so to speak, and push on through to victory.

The sport of boxing serves as a good illustration. Many times a boxer will have to take a punch (or let himself get hit) in order to deliver the knock-out punch.

As we travel down the road we are walking with God, sometimes we think we'll never have any trials or problems. We think that because we're walking with God, everything should be fine as we go along. But I want you to understand that if you're walking in the will of God, doing what He wants you to do, you're going to encounter some opposition at some time or another.

You're not just going to walk through life without opposition. The devil does not like the Word of God, and he will oppose you every time you start believing God for anything. The devil will oppose you at every turn. He will be there to jump on your shoulder, so to speak, and tell you that you can't make it.

I want you to think back and notice that when you were attacked in your finances, your health, or some other part of your life, the opposition came at a time when you were believing God and quoting the Word. When you say what God's Word says, you may get attacked—many times by religious people.

You may have found that to be true when you started living by faith, believing the Bible for what the Bible said, and leaving some of your religious traditions in your former place of worship.

Maybe some religious people didn't want anything to do with you. They may have even called you names. I know some people call "word of faith" charismatics the "name-it-and-claim-it" or the "confess-it-and-possess-it" bunch. That's all right with me; I like those titles. They sound as though people in that group are getting something. I'm interested in possessing. I'm interested in having everything that God's Word says is mine!

I'm not talking about someone's church creed or doctrine. I'm talking about what the Bible says. We cannot afford to allow anyone to cause us to quit believing what the Bible says.

Holy Ghost Power

In the Book of Acts, we read about a man who set an example of what kind of attitude we should have. Stephen had an attitude that caused him to serve and believe God, no matter what.

ACTS 6:8–11 (*NIV*)

8 Now Stephen, a man full of God's grace and power, did great wonders and miraculous signs among the people.

9 Opposition arose, however, from members of the Synagogue of the Freedmen (as it was called)—Jews of

Cyrene and Alexandria as well as the provinces of Cilicia and Asia. These men began to argue with Stephen,

10 **but they could not stand up against his wisdom or the Spirit by whom he spoke.**

11 **Then they secretly persuaded some men to say, "We have heard Stephen speak words of blasphemy against Moses and against God."**

ACTS 7:54–55 (NIV)

54 **When they** [the people] **heard this, they were furious and gnashed their teeth at him** [Stephen].

55 **But Stephen, full of the Holy Spirit, looked up to heaven and saw the glory of God, and Jesus standing at the right hand of God.**

Acts 6:9 says opposition arose against Stephen from members of the Synagogue of the Freedmen, a Jewish sect comprised of Jews from Cyrene, Alexandria, Cilicia, and the provinces of Asia.

Notice Acts 6:10: *"But they* [the religious people] *could not stand up against his* [Stephen's] *wisdom or the Spirit by whom he spoke."* If you are walking in line with God's Word and speaking God's Word to the situations around you, no opposition will be able to stand against you. No weapon formed against you will prosper (Isa. 54:17)!

Notice again that Acts 6:10 says, *"But they could not stand up against his wisdom or the Spirit by whom he spoke."* This verse doesn't mean that Stephen talked *about* the Holy Spirit. It means that everything Stephen said was prompted and empowered *by* the Holy Spirit!

In Acts chapter 4, Peter and John were "called on the carpet" by the religious leaders for doing good and healing a man who had been sitting at the gate of the temple. When the lame man was healed, he went about the temple running and leaping and praising God.

When Peter and John spoke at the trial, the people asked, "How are these men able to speak this way, since they are ignorant and uneducated?" Peter and John spoke the way they did because the Holy Spirit gave them utterance.

You see, the Holy Spirit is stronger than the spirit of rebellion. The Holy Spirit is stronger than the spirit of opposition. The Holy Spirit is stronger than religious spirits. The Holy Spirit is stronger than any kind of spirit.

It's Time to 'Cop an Attitude'!

The Holy Spirit is number one! And if you will allow Him to flow and live big in your life, you will develop an attitude that will cause you to never turn and run. You will have an attitude that will cause you to stand fast on your confession of the Word of God.

You can't just confess *anything*. Your confession must be based on the Word of God. If God said it, you have a right to say it—the Bible tells us so.

Our attitude should be one that says, *"If God tells me to do something, then regardless of the circumstances, I will do it, and I will stand fast. I won't turn and run."*

Stephen displayed an attitude of meekness when he refused to fight back or defend himself physically, but many times we overlook the most important attitude he had because we're engaged in admiring his meekness—his doing what was right and not lashing out. Notice Stephen was able to stand firm and do what was right because he had the attitude, "I have done what God called me to do, and I will not relent."

If we're going to be victorious as we live for God, we're going to have to have that same kind of an attitude. We need the attitude that says, "This is what God has called me to do, and come what may, here I will stand! I will walk in the ways of the Word of God. I will walk in love. I will confess what God says belongs to me, and I will have the victory that is mine."

One day you may find yourself in a position like the one Stephen found himself in when everything was against him.

You may find yourself in a position where it looks as though everything is against you. In that situation, you have to decide what kind of attitude you're going to have.

We've all heard the phrase "copping an attitude." Now it's time to decide what kind of attitude we're going to "cop." Are we going to take on the attitude that says, "Well, I thought God was in this. This is what God's Word said to do, but now I don't know"? Or are we going to take on the attitude that boldly proclaims, "God said it, I believe it, and that settles it! I am following the will of God no matter what!"? The first kind of attitude will get you absolutely nowhere. The second attitude will bring you victory.

Whether a Christian has the first or second attitude doesn't determine whether or not he will go to Heaven. A Christian who is trusting Jesus as Savior will spend eternity with God whether or not he is strong in faith or in spirit. But the one who goes to Heaven after living a life of hard times will not have much to show for it. I'm interested in going to Heaven having received in life all the benefits that belong to me. I'm not interested in letting any benefit that belongs to me according to the Word of God go untouched. I'm going to use my faith to take the future—and I'm talking about *this* life—by storm.

Fellowship on Common Ground

What we believe about faith in God's Word to receive His blessings will always affect us in this life, but it will not necessarily determine whether or not we go to Heaven. I don't let issues not central to salvation keep me from fellowshipping with other believers who may not believe as I do. Some people are always getting into religious arguments. I've had people ask me, "Why did you fellowship with So-and-so? Don't you know what he believes about such-and-such?" Friend, I will fellowship with anyone who believes in being born again by the blood of the Lord Jesus Christ and in living right before God. It doesn't matter what he believes about healing. It doesn't matter what he believes about the baptism in the Holy Spirit. It doesn't matter what he believes about prosperity. I can fellowship with others around the fact that they believe in being born again by the blood of the Lord Jesus Christ!

We need to learn to fellowship with one another and not "fall out" or get into strife over disagreements. The Bible tells us not to let offense have any place in our lives. Just because someone is a little different from you or believes a little differently than the way you believe is no reason to get into strife. The only requisite for going to Heaven is being born again by the blood of the Lord Jesus Christ.

Many Christians want to argue over water baptism. It doesn't matter to me whether you were immersed in a baptismal pool, a pond, a running river, or whether you had a bucket poured over your head. The only thing I want to know is, have you been blood-washed? If you have been born again, washed in the blood of the Lord Jesus Christ, I can fellowship with you!

That's the attitude of love. We do not have to see eye-to-eye on every subject in order to fellowship with one another. We need to be careful about being offended so easily. We need to be careful about judging others and not say they do not belong to the Body of Christ because they don't believe like we do.

This is an issue that Paul talks about in the last part of First Corinthians Chapter 11.

1 CORINTHIANS 11:27–31

27 **Wherefore whosoever shall eat this bread, and drink this cup of the Lord, unworthily, shall be guilty of the body and blood of the Lord.**

28 **But let a man examine himself, and so let him eat of that bread, and drink of that cup.**

29 **For he that eateth and drinketh unworthily, eateth and drinketh damnation to himself, NOT DISCERNING THE LORD'S BODY.**

30 **For this cause many are weak and sickly among you, and many sleep.**

31 For if we would judge ourselves, we should not be judged.

One way we don't discern the Lord's Body (verse 29) is by not recognizing the whole Body of Christ. Just because you don't see eye-to-eye with someone on some minor subject does not mean he or she isn't a member of the Body of Christ. We need to stay with the Gospel of the Lord Jesus Christ and continue to walk in love, "discerning the Lord's Body."

When you find yourself in situations in which you don't see eye-to-eye with someone, just continue to have an attitude of love. And keep the attitude that says, "I cannot be defeated, and I will not quit!" No matter what others say, don't stop believing God's Word and walking in love. You will never be defeated in life with that kind of attitude.

Quitters Never Win

The only way you can be a failure in life is if you fail at something and then refuse to pick yourself up, so to speak, and go on. Until you refuse to go on, you have only failed at that particular thing you attempted. A person can *fail*, but that doesn't make him a *failure*! Even if you get knocked down, you aren't a failure unless you stay down. If you get up and go on with your life, you're not a failure. God is not looking for perfect people! He's looking for people who are willing to say, "I'm going to follow God no matter what."

If you happen to be in a situation in which you have messed up, just repent and say, "Lord, I've messed up. Please forgive me." Then ask anyone else you need to ask to forgive you too. And then get up, move on, and don't look back.

Too many people "camp out" where they failed. That's a bad place to stay because you are wallowing in sorrow and self-pity, saying, "Well, if it hadn't been for such-and-such, I wouldn't be in this mess." If you want to take your future by storm and be a success for God, then get up, stomp out the campfire ashes, strike the tent, pack up the equipment, and move on for God!

Stand Fast!

I can remember what my father used to say every time my family faced a problem. Regardless of what the problem was, my dad would say, "This is just another opportunity to prove that the Word of God works." That's the kind of attitude you need to have when you're facing a problem.

You can look at your problem and say, "Oh, what am I going to do now?" Or you can look at the problem in light of the Word of God and say, "This is just another opportunity for me to prove that God's Word works!"

You might be facing some obstacles today. Stand strong on God's Word! Move forward, living in line with God's Word. Forget the past; forget what lies behind you. Forget who said what, and remember what God said. Galatians 5:1 says, *"Stand fast therefore in the liberty wherewith Christ hath made us free, and be not entangled again with the yoke of bondage."*

When people were mad at Stephen and were coming against him with everything they had, Stephen developed a certain attitude. He stood firm in his convictions of what God said. He dared to stand for God, and he died for God, having pleased Him with his faith.

We may never have to die for our beliefs, yet sometimes we may feel as though we will. But if we're going to be successful, we have to bear up underneath whatever we face. I'm not saying we are to lie down and just accept the negative circumstances. But we shouldn't cave in, either, when circumstances bear down on us to try to get us off our faith. Paul told us that there is no temptation—test, trial, tribulation, or problem—that will come your way that God has not given you the grace to come through on the other side (1 Cor. 10:13).

Right now, you may be in a situation in which there is darkness on every side. Life may look bleak, and you may be saying to yourself, *I don't see any way out. I see no hope!* This is where you have to stand fast with the attitude, "I shall prevail by the Word of God. Standing on the promises of God, I shall prevail. In the face of every obstacle that says 'no,' *I will prevail!*"

Someone may say, "I'm surveying the horizon, but I don't see anything except darkness and bleakness." Remember, that's looking with your natural eyes. Begin to look with your spiritual eyes, and you will discover that the forces of evil are no match for the forces of God! Begin to look and see that the Lord is good and that the righteous are never forsaken and should never have to beg for bread (Ps. 34:8; Ps. 37:25). Stand fast, and maintain the attitude of faith that says, "I cannot be defeated, and I will not quit!"

Exercise and Build Your Faith

I was raised in a home where faith was taught, lived, and demonstrated. Growing up, I saw my father exercise his faith in all kinds of circumstances. I watched my father sell the only car we had and get to his meetings the best way he could. He would ride a bus, hitchhike, and do whatever it took to get to the church. Most people don't know that about my dad. Everyone sees where he is today financially, and they want to have what he has. But go back a few years, and see how he got to where he is today. If you want to have what he has, you'd better learn to walk the faith walk that he walked.

I have never seen my dad's attitude of faith falter in the least. He has learned to walk by faith in the Word of God regardless of what happens around him. I've often heard him tell the story about the time he and my mom were discussing not being fretful or anxious.

Mom said, "I don't believe you would worry if the kids and I fell dead right here."

My dad said, in effect, "Certainly not. Wouldn't that be a stupid thing to do? The Bible says, 'Which of you by taking thought can add one cubit unto your stature?' [Matt. 6:27]. Certainly I wouldn't worry about it. If all of you were dead, why would I worry then? You'd already be in Heaven!"

No matter how bad the situation might have been, my dad's attitude never changed. Even when he had to sell his car, my dad kept holding meetings and telling the people that God wants to prosper His children.

When I was in the third grade, we moved into a three-room duplex. There was a living room, a bedroom, and a kitchen. I slept on a roll-away bed either on the back porch or in the kitchen, depending on the time of the year. My sister and my cousin, who lived with us at the time, slept on a hide-a-bed in the living room. Of course, my parents shared the bedroom.

The back porch where I slept in the summer was screened in and was shared by both duplex tenants. There was a bathroom on each side of the porch. So when the people came out of the other house to go to their bathroom, they came into my bedroom! Of course, in the winter I put the roll-away bed in the kitchen. There was never any sleeping late for me. I always had to get up early and get out of the way!

When I was in the eighth grade, we moved into a house, and I had my own bedroom. That was a great day, and I will never forget how we got that house. When my dad first saw the house, he knew in his spirit it was going to be his house. So he walked around the property and claimed it as ours. At first the people who owned the property told my dad they didn't want to sell. My dad's attitude never changed. He didn't tell them, but he kept saying, "They want to sell; they just don't know it yet."

My dad just kept believing God. And I never will forget, one day he came in from a meeting with an envelope in his hand. He handed me that envelope and said, "Count what's inside." I had done that before because sometimes the church where he ministered gave him the offering in an envelope. So I opened the envelope, and I counted ten one-hundred-dollar bills. It was the first time I had ever seen a hundred-dollar bill. That money helped us get the house.

My dad's attitude didn't change *before* we got that money, and it didn't change *after* we got that money. His attitude was already set long before we actually got the house. He knew that house would be ours, so he exercised his faith and kept confessing what he believed.

No Overnight Success

Even when we are in faith, we don't always get what we are believing for right away. We have to mix patience with faith. Hebrews 6:12 says that it's through faith *and* patience that we inherit the promises of God. And James 1:3 tells us that the trying of our faith works patience.

There will be opposition when you are living for God. You must learn to have the attitude that the devil cannot win! But I want you to realize that the people you see now who have strong faith and seem to always have the victory have been living by faith and walking with God for many years. They didn't get to where they are now overnight, and they walked through the same kind of trials and tribulations that you walk through. Many have driven "junk" cars and have lived in houses where the curtains blew away from the window on a windy day even when the windows were closed! I've been there. My wife and I lived in one of those houses when my son Craig was an infant. When he was born, I had to redo the room to try to keep him warm.

Don't look at where I am now and think I was born with a silver spoon in my mouth, so to speak. My dad gave me the only silver spoon I ever had, and it was the Word of God! He told me, "Son, study the Word. Learn how to walk with God and live for God. Do what He says no matter what comes or what goes. If you'll do that, you will come out on top every time! The Apostle Paul said God *always* causes us to triumph in Christ Jesus [2 Cor. 2:14]."

Friend, no matter where you are in life—no matter what you're facing or how many problems you have—if you will get hold of God's Word, believe it, and make right decisions based on the Word, you will develop the attitude, "I'm going through to victory no matter what!" And God will bring you out and cause you to triumph!

Notice I said you must make right decisions. We can't afford to make stupid decisions. You see, many people bring things on themselves because they make bad decisions. Then they want to blame God or the devil for the situation they're in, but it's not God's fault or the devil's fault. If we make bad decisions, the consequences are *our* fault. We need to use our head! But even when we make bad decisions, God in His mercy is there to help us.

True Grit

Again, to be a success in life, you have to have a certain kind of attitude. You have to have grit. According to the dictionary, "grit" means *firmness of mind or spirit; unyielding courage in the face of hardship or danger.* We call it "guts" down in Texas. It's the attitude that says, "Neither the devil nor anyone else is going to keep me from getting what God said belongs to me!"

I want to tell you a little secret. It's not up to God what you receive in life—it's up to you! You can allow the devil to steal from you if you want to. But if you'll learn to take the Word of God for what it says with the attitude, "God said it; I believe it; that settles it," you can live victoriously in this life. Walk with God's Word spilling from your mouth, and live in line with it. Walk in love, speak in love, and live in love. When you walk by faith and love, God will see you through to victory!

Only you can determine what kind of attitude you will have. Determine right now to have the kind of attitude that says, "No matter what, I'm going through to victory!"

The Bible says that no weapon formed against you will prosper (Isa. 54:17). Believe it! Act like it! Walk down the road of life confessing God's Word. Speak to your problem and say, "No! It will not be that way." Speak what God says and say, "That obstacle in my life will fall. The crooked place shall be made straight [Luke 3:5]. And I shall walk to victory as I confess God's Word. With the shield of faith for my protection, I will move forward into the battle, knowing that it's not my battle but God's [2 Chron. 20:15]. And God never loses. Therefore I will come out victorious on the other side."

You can make a heartfelt, positive confession of God's Word anytime, even at mealtime. For example, every time we pray over our meals, we can thank God for the benefits in His Word. After we ask God to bless the food, we can say, "We thank You for taking sickness away from our midst and for giving us health and healing. Thank You that no weapon formed against us will prosper." Every time we do that, we are confessing God's Word over our lives. When my dad prays for the food, he says the same thing: "Thank You for taking sickness away from us and for giving us health and healing."

I've stood with my dad in the hour of sorrow when loved ones passed away. I've been with him when he didn't understand why he couldn't pray the prayer of faith for some of them. And I've stood there with him as he watched them draw their last breath. From inside his spirit came these words: *"O death, where is thy sting? O grave, where is thy victory?"* (1 Cor. 15:55). And then scripture after scripture after scripture began to roll out of him.

That's the kind of attitude it takes to be a success in life. If you want to take your future by storm, get hold of the Word. Get the attitude that no matter what you face, you are going on with God. Believe God and confess the Word no matter what happens. No matter who dies, no matter who falls, no matter who says or does what! Go with God, and you'll find yourself on the victory side every time.

Chapter 6

Set Your Sights

Problems are those things we see when we take our eyes off the goal.

John Maxwell

━━ ⚔ ━━

When it comes to taking our future by storm, we've seen that attitudes are very important. One reason attitudes are so important is because they can dictate what kind of life we will live.

A person's attitude will actually set the tone of his or her environment. We must understand that it's one thing to talk about believing God and living a life committed to God, but it's another to have an attitude that constantly demonstrates and backs up what we are saying.

Many people talk about commitment, but you can tell by the way they talk and act that their heart isn't in it. We may not use the term "attitude." Instead, we say, "He may be doing such and such, but his heart's not in it." How can you tell when people's hearts aren't in what they're saying or doing? By their attitude.

It's easy to tell when a person says yes to something, but he really wanted to say no to it. Maybe at one time or another, you have said yes to something that you really wanted to say no to, and you thought you hid the truth from the other person. Most of the time the other person will not say anything, but he or she knows that you said yes begrudgingly. Your attitude usually gives you away.

Maybe the reason some people don't want to follow our Christian lead is that we're saying one thing with our mouth but revealing something else with our attitude.

Don't Be Deceived

In Luke chapter 21, Jesus talks about His Second Coming. From this passage, we can learn about several of the attitudes we are supposed to maintain as we anticipate Jesus' return.

LUKE 21:8

8 And he [Jesus] said, Take heed that ye be not deceived: for many shall come in my name, saying, I am Christ; and the time draweth near: go ye not therefore after them.

Jesus told His followers to beware of impostors who will try to lead them astray. Reading this passage, we recognize other things we need to beware in the area of deception.

For example, often it's easy to recognize falsehood when people openly speak against God or Jesus, but it is more difficult to recognize imposters who closely resemble the real thing.

One deception we may have to deal with is in the area of doctrine. Just ignore anyone who tries to preach a doctrine that doesn't line up with the Word of God. Overlook it and go on with your life. The Apostle Paul said it this way: *"But though we, or an angel from heaven, preach any other gospel unto you than that which we have preached unto you, let him be accursed"* (Gal. 1:8). In other words, don't pay any attention to what is said if it doesn't agree with God's Word; just go on believing God's Word.

Don't worry about how to answer people who oppose the Gospel that you believe. Go on believing what you believe and let them write and say what they want to. What they say and do doesn't change anything as far as you're concerned. The only way that it can affect you is if you let it. Don't ever let anything hinder you from accomplishing what you need to accomplish for God.

LUKE 21:14

14 Settle it therefore in your hearts, not to meditate before what ye shall answer.

We simply need to find out what God's Word says and walk on down the road of life with the truth of His Word in our heart.

The Bible repeatedly warns us not to believe every doctrine that comes along. Ephesians 4:14 reveals God's desire *"that we henceforth be no more children, tossed to and fro, and carried about with every wind of doctrine, by the sleight of men, and cunning craftiness, whereby they lie in wait to deceive."* We know from this scripture that some doctrine can be deceptive.

False doctrine has just enough scripture in it that if you aren't extremely perceptive, it can look correct. In the Word of God, we read that even the devil quotes scripture (Matt. 4:6; Luke 4:10)! But because we are born again, we have the Holy Spirit within us to guide us into all truth (John 16:13).

You should be spiritually perceptive enough not to be deceived, but if at some point you discover that you've missed it, don't be afraid to say, "God, I missed it." The person who hasn't ever messed up and missed it can throw the first stone, but if people are honest, no stones will be thrown.

When it comes to not being deceived or taken in, Paul's advice to Timothy is good advice for us to follow.

2 TIMOTHY 4:2–3

2 Preach the word; be instant in season, out of season; reprove, rebuke, exhort with all longsuffering and doctrine.

3 For the time will come when they will not endure sound doctrine; but after their own lusts shall they heap to themselves teachers, having itching ears.

I have already talked briefly about people with "itching ears." There are some people who are beyond help already. They will only listen to those people who teach what they want to hear. Some Christians only want to hear messages on prosperity and having a good time in the Lord. If the pastor mentions anything about tests or trials or teaches on subjects such as judgment or self-control, they close their ears and go to church somewhere else.

Many Christians today want to have a shouting service or have the gifts of the Spirit in operation every time they go to church. But the gifts of the Spirit only operate as the Spirit wills. That's why it's important to preach the Word. You can *always* preach the Word, and the Word *always* works!

Unfortunately, in the natural, there are people who, given the chance, would eat sweets until they died of malnutrition. If you only ate cake, candy, and ice cream and avoided eating meats and fruits and vegetables, you would not live a very healthy, productive life.

Similarly, there are people who, spiritually speaking, want to only "eat sweets." But just as we must have a well-balanced diet in the natural, we must also have a well-balanced spiritual diet in order to live a healthy, productive spiritual life. It's okay to shout and dance and run, but we can't live on that. Always come back to the Word. That is our foundation.

We need to be careful that our attitude doesn't get to the point where we're always searching for something else that's new and missing out on the real move of God.

God is looking for people who are faithful and committed. God judges people on their faithfulness, not on how high they jump, how many times they dance in the spirit, how well they sing or preach, or how many tapes or books they sell. God judges on faithfulness. Numbers don't make anyone a success. You are a success with God when you're committed and faithful to His Word and to His plan for your life.

Don't Be Disturbed

Luke 21:8 warns us about deception; verse 9 warns us about fear. God's Word tells us that we're not to be disturbed by the latest news or by what we see happening around us. Luke 21: 9 says, "When you hear of wars and revolutions, *do not be frightened.* These things must happen first, but the end will not come right away" (*NIV*).

People are often fearful about all the natural things that are happening in the world: the stock market, tornadoes, floods, earthquakes, and wars. News of these things doesn't bother me in the least. I don't even get upset over it. On nights when I hear that there is a tornado warning, I just take authority over my personal property and over everything that RHEMA owns because I have jurisdiction over those things. Then I go back to sleep trusting in the Lord. When you hear of natural disasters or rumors of some pending catastrophe, take authority over what belongs to *you.* You can't take authority over what belongs to someone else, but you *can* take authority over what is yours.

We don't need to get upset. Some people are always upset because of the signs of the times that they see coming to pass all around them. People's hearts are failing for fear, but we don't have to be afraid. We serve a mighty God!

You may hear that the price of fuel is going up, that you're going to have the worst winter ever, or that taxes are getting higher. But you don't have to let bad news affect you. Instead of being upset, worried, or afraid, you can settle down and be confident that God is still God and He will always be God.

God took care of more than two million Israelites in the desert after He delivered them from Egypt's bondage. Everything under the sun, so to speak, threatened them, but God provided for them and protected them. God gave them water to drink when there wasn't any water. God gave them food to eat when there wasn't any food. That's the God I'm serving. And if God can take care of two million, He can certainly take care of *you— and He will!*

Too many people become so fearful of all of these natural things that are taking place. But when I see all these things happening, I'm reminded of what God's Word says: "*. . . when*

*these things begin to come to pass, then look up, and lift up your heads;
FOR YOUR REDEMPTION DRAWETH NIGH"* (Luke 21:28).

This passage also talk about end-time events, things that will
happen in the earth before Christ returns. We don't have to be
disturbed by news of any of these things happening because
Luke 21:28 tells us we can look up—our redemption draws nigh.
We have to have faith and believe that. These signs simply
encourage us for we know that Jesus is coming back soon.

Not only can we stay in peace regardless of the international
news, but we can stay in peace when we hear all sorts news
concerning what's happening in different church circles.

Some people get all excited and anxious, saying, "Have you
heard what So-and-so is preaching? We need to do something
about it!" No, we don't. When you know the truth, you don't
get upset over any kind of bad news—secular or religious.

Someone might say, "Oh, but haven't you heard what's
going on?" It doesn't make any difference. God is my source,
and His Word is truth.

With God You Cannot Fail

When the devil comes against you, you don't have to be
disturbed. The devil hasn't won! As a matter of fact, he lost
more than 2,000 years ago! Instead of wringing your hands and
saying, "Oh, what am I going to do now?" begin to speak the
Word and remind the devil of what Jesus has done.

And in the meantime, check your attitude. Examine the
way you're thinking about things. The way you think about
what you've heard from God's Word will determine what you
believe and speak.

The Word of God has a lot to say about keeping the proper
attitude. The proper attitude keeps you in the proper frame of
mind. The proper frame of mind keeps you thinking correctly.
Right thinking brings right believing. Right believing brings right
speaking, and right speaking brings positive results. Wrong thinking
creates doubt and unbelief, which bring negative results.

With God you cannot fail. As long as you keep going with God you can't fail. According to your circumstances, it may seem as though you're going to fail, but you can't fail! The only way circumstances can triumph over you is if you quit.

Make a decision today and determine that you will not be deceived or disturbed by anything but, instead, you will set your sights on God and on what He's called you to do.

Stand on the Word!

So far, I've dealt with the negative side of attitudes and what *not* to do: Don't be deceived; don't be disturbed. But there is a positive side too. We must realize that we've been redeemed. We have to stand on the promises of God's Word come what may—no matter what happens or what anyone says.

When believing for healing, for finances, or for anything else, stand on what the Word says. God's Word tells us that Jesus already defeated the devil. That means that now Satan is under our feet!

When the devil tries to come against you, make your stand and say, "That is far enough!" Let his threats and negative thoughts roll off you "like water off of a duck's back." In other words, if we're standing on the Word, then problems or threats just roll off of us without ever harming us.

I'm reminded of a product that is now being sold to use on car windshields. After it's sprayed on the glass, any rain that hits the windshield just "beads up" and rolls off the glass. That's what the Word of God will do for us. As we saturate ourselves in the Word, when the devil or something negative comes against us, the circumstances just bead up and roll off us, so to speak.

Some people are afraid of the devil. When the devil knows people are afraid of him, he takes advantage of them. If you know anything about riding a horse, you know that a horse can tell when its rider is afraid. That horse won't do anything you want him to do if he knows you're afraid of him. If you don't show him who's boss, he'll take you back to the barn while everyone else is trotting down the road. The devil is the same way. Until you show him that you're the "boss" and let him know that you're not afraid of him, he's going to take advantage of you every time you turn around.

The Bible says that no weapon formed against you shall prosper (Isa. 54:17). The devil can form a weapon, but it's just a smokescreen. All he can do is talk because he doesn't have any "bite" to his bark! Just like some dogs bark and growl and act like they're going to tear your leg off, the devil is barking and growling. But when you stomp your foot and resist the devil with the Word of God, he goes running in terror like a whipped pup (James 4:7)!

Start standing on the promises of God's Word, and make up your mind that your feet are going to stay planted on the Rock.

Chapter 7

The Importance of Patience

Our patience will achieve more than our force.

Edmund Burke

In the previous chapter, we used Luke chapter 21 as our guide for talking about attitudes. That passage in Luke is actually talking about the second coming of Jesus and our attitudes toward His return, but I'm using the passage to deal with our attitudes in general.

We've talked about being deceived by impostors and about being disturbed by bad news. We've talked about the importance of not worrying about how to answer people who don't believe exactly the way we do and who give us a hard time. And we've talked about not being fearful of natural disasters, financial upheaval, or other bad news.

I want to continue studying the importance of attitudes, namely the attitude of patience. We must be patient as we await the Lord's return and as we go about our everyday lives. Luke 21:19 says, *"In your patience possess ye your souls."* The *New International Version* says, "By standing firm you will gain life."

We live in an impatient world, and we all have to work on being patient. I want you to realize that I'm just like anyone else. I'm still working on me. Anyone who says that he has already achieved perfection and is no longer working to improve is not telling the truth. There was only one Perfect One, and He was crucified!

Most people will agree that one of the hardest things we have to learn is patience. On the road, people tend to get impatient with other drivers (especially if they're in a hurry to get somewhere). And people get impatient with their children, waiters, store clerks, and so forth.

We even get impatient waiting for the manifestation of answered prayer. We get impatient when we're standing in faith, and, if we're not careful, impatience will push us over into unbelief. Many people don't realize it, but by being impatient, they let the devil push them out of the arena of faith into the arena of unbelief.

One indication that we are being impatient with the Lord is when we start complaining and whining to Him. You might say, "I would never do such a thing!" But when we question Him, saying, "Lord, why haven't You already done such and such? I don't understand why You haven't already done it," we are in unbelief.

Patience is so important because without it, we won't be able to stay in faith. As I said previously, Hebrews 6:12 tells us that it's through faith and patience that we inherit the promises of God.

The Lord Is Patient

Throughout the Scriptures, we read about the Lord's patience and longsuffering. James 5:7 says He is waiting for the precious fruit of the earth and He has *long patience* for it. Second Peter 3:9 says, "The Lord is not slow in keeping his promise, as some understand slowness. He is patient with you, not wanting anyone to perish, but everyone to come to repentance" (*NIV*).

It would greatly benefit us if we would practice patience. It seems as though the attitude in today's world is, "Hurry up! Hurry up! Hurry up!" If we're not careful, we will begin to let impatience negatively affect our faith in the Word of God.

Have you ever noticed that when you start getting impatient in one area, it affects every other area of your life? You let impatience begin to dominate and the next thing you know, you become impatient with those around you. You don't really mean to be that way, and when you stop yourself and think how in the world you got to that place, you realize it all started with impatience in some other area.

A Daily Dose of Patience

We live in a natural world. The physical body in which we live contacts the natural world continually. Our natural body doesn't contact the spiritual world. It's the man on the inside who has all of the fruits of the Spirit mentioned in Galatians chapter 5. And one of those fruits is patience.

Because patience is a fruit of the Spirit, we know if we're born again, we have the fruit of patience within us. But, you see, the old man on the outside doesn't want any part of patience. He rejects the fruits all the time, but we have to let what's inside us come to the outside and dominate our life. We have to tell ourselves on a daily basis, "You are going to be patient."

You have to do that every day—sometimes several times a day! In that way, patience is similar to some of the vitamins that we take, such as vitamin C. Because some vitamins aren't stored in the body, we have to take a daily dose for them to do us good. Even then, you shouldn't rely just on vitamins. No, throughout the day, you are supposed to eat different foods that contain that particular vitamin.

That is sort of the way it is with patience. We tell ourselves to be patient, and we are—for a time. But then just a little while later, when we need patience, we find we need another intake.

Turn Your Thoughts Heavenward

So far, we have learned that we need to have patience as we are walking here in this natural world and as we look for the coming of the Lord Jesus Christ. Another thing we need to do as we look for the coming of the Lord Jesus is to turn our thoughts heavenward.

When we encounter different situations, circumstances, and trials, we must remember that the answer to our problem is not on this earth. If the answer to your problem was on this earth, you would have already taken care of that problem. So what you need to do is look up!

Luke 21:28 says, *"And when these things begin to come to pass, then look up, and lift up your heads; for your redemption draweth nigh."* Of course, the "things" Jesus is talking about are mentioned in the previous verses, but we can apply this verse to anything that happens in our life. For instance, when you begin to see circumstances and obstacles blocking your way, don't look at what's going on and say, "Oh what's going to happen now?" Instead, begin to look up, because your redemption comes from on High!

Another word for "redemption" is "deliverance." So we could say, "Your deliverance comes from on High." Remember, God is Your Deliverer, and your deliverance is going to come from Him, not from some person.

Arm of the Flesh or Hand of God?

When faced with troubling circumstances, many people want to say, "If only I could have Brother or Sister So-and-so pray for me." Or they say, "If I could just go over to such and such prayer group, I know I'd receive my answer."

If you look to a person to receive deliverance, you won't receive anything. Now don't misunderstand what I'm saying. I realize that we can pray for one another and agree with one another in prayer according to the Word of God. The point I'm trying to make is, we must always recognize and understand that our redemption comes from *God*–no matter who does the praying.

Many people go to healing and deliverance meetings because of the minister who's going to be there. And very often they get upset if the minister they went to see has someone else pray for the sick that night.

I've been in meetings where Brother Hagin decided to have me, my son, or a member of the RHEMA Singers and Band pray for the sick. I've seen some people actually get mad because they wanted Brother Hagin to pray for them.

Years ago when I was crusade director, a man at one of the meetings got very angry because Brother Hagin wasn't the one laying hands on the sick the night this man came to the meeting. He was so mad that Brother Hagin didn't pray for folks that he came and cussed me out.

I just stood there and looked at him, because it sort of took me by surprise. Finally, I said, "Well, you wouldn't have received anything, anyway, with that kind of an attitude."

When he got defensive, I asked, "Who are you expecting to heal you—God or Brother Hagin?"

Sometimes people don't realize it and without thinking or being consciously aware, they look to other people to get their answers for them when they could get their answer praying for themselves.

I can remember one man saying, "I've called every prayer and intercession group in the whole United States that I know anything about, so I know I'm going to get deliverance."

I asked him, "Who are you expecting to deliver you? God or all those people who are praying?"

We need to view people as being the vessel that God works through—the instrument through which the power of God can flow, keeping in mind that *God* is the Healer, Deliverer, and Redeemer! So it makes no difference whether it's a nine-year-old child or a well-known minister praying for you. If they're both born again, God can move through either of them!

Lift Up Your Head!

Now is the time to lift up your head and be confident. We need to be as persuaded that God will deliver us as the Apostle Paul was when he said, "I know whom I have believed" (2 Tim. 1:12).

Many times people who have a bad attitude walk around with their head down. I can easily discern when Christians have a negative attitude; I can tell they're down about things by the way they carry themselves. If someone always walks with his head down and shoulders slumped, it might be because he has lost his confidence. Hebrews 10:35 says, "Cast not away your confidence."

Some Christians lose their confidence because someone they know didn't receive what he was believing God for. Friend, let me tell you something. It doesn't matter if everyone in the world believes and doesn't receive, I'm still going to be confident in God's Word. I'm still going to hold my head up and say with a confident attitude, "God is my Deliverer and my Redeemer!"

Now I'm not talking about being confident in *yourself*; that's being conceited. The Word of God tells us not to think of ourselves more highly than we ought" (Rom. 12:3). I'm talking about being confident in God and in His Word.

However, as a side note, Romans 12:3 doesn't tell you not to think of yourself *at all*. It just says don't think more highly than you ought to think.

Some people say, "Oh no, you shouldn't ever think of yourself," and in their so-called humility, they become prideful.

They say, "I am nothing. I'm just a sinner saved by grace."

If you've been born again, then you're no longer a sinner saved by grace. You are a new creature in Christ Jesus (2 Cor. 5:17)! You are now a child of God and one of the redeemed!

Do You Know Who You Are?

Often people who don't have any confidence don't know who they are; they are searching for who they are. Well, I'm not searching for who I am. I'm confident of who I am. I am one of the redeemed. I am one of the called-out ones. I am one who is a part of the Body of Christ and a member of the family of God. My name's written in the Lamb's Book of Life.

I'm confident of the fact that if I live for God and walk with God, He will lead, guide, and direct me. He will make the crooked place straight, the low place high, and the high place level (Luke 3:5). He'll break down the gates of iron and brass (Isa. 45:2) and remove anything else that blocks my path. All I have to do is walk with Him and be confident in Him and in what He can do!

Lift up your head, because your redemption draweth nigh. "Redemption draweth nigh" is the *King James Version*. Another translation reads, "Your deliverance is at hand." So be confident in God's delivering power.

When I begin to feel surrounded on every side and it seems as though everything is "crashing" in on me, I stop myself and say, "Wait a minute. Here comes my deliverance."

If you keep looking at the problem, the pressures, and the circumstances, everything just seems to get worse and worse. But when you lift up your head, you no longer see problems, pressures, and circumstances. You see the redemption of God that belongs to you.

Faint Not!

Jesus Christ *is* coming again. But as we await His return with patience, there are things God's Word tells us to do in the meantime.

For instance, we should be concerned about our personal life and spiritual welfare. Luke 21:34 says, "*. . . take heed to yourselves, lest at any time your hearts be overcharged with surfeiting . . . and cares of this life . . . .*" And Galatians 6:9 tells us not to grow weary in well doing.

GALATIANS 6:9
9   And let us not be weary in well doing: for in due season we shall reap, IF WE FAINT NOT.

If you're not careful, you can become weary in well doing. In due season we will reap, but only if we faint not.

Stay Ready

Another thing we need to do as we patiently await the Lord's return is to watch and pray.

LUKE 21:36

36 Watch ye therefore, and pray always, that ye may be accounted worthy to escape all these things that shall come to pass, and to stand before the Son of man.

I always try to stay watchful, or observant, and notice what is going on around me. I notice what's going on in the spiritual world, and I notice what's going on in the natural world. Then I study the Word of God to see what it says about living in the last days. That's how I keep myself ready.

Paul says to pray without ceasing (1 Thess. 5:17). Now that doesn't mean you stay on bended knee all day. I mean, you have to work *sometime*. The point is, you can have a prayer in your heart while you're working. You can pray while you're driving down the street.

As a teenager, I used to go out in the garage and work on cars a lot. I prayed and meditated on the Word while I tinkered on my car. I got a lot of sermons out there working on my cars. I would get a thought and have to stop working, wipe the grease off my hands, and write it down.

You can pray while you're walking or jogging. Many people put headphones on to listen to music while they're exercising. Instead of listening to music, they could be praying while they're exercising.

Reflections of Jesus

We must be mindful that Jesus is coming again. But we also need to be mindful of what kind of attitudes we have while we are awaiting His return. We are called to present a Christ-like attitude at *all* times to *all* people *everywhere*. When we have the right attitude, we can often witness to people without ever opening our mouth. May it never be said that our attitude made someone not want to follow Jesus.

Remember your attitude affects what you do and reflects who you are. If you have a bad attitude, you reflect a negative image. If you have a good attitude, you reflect a positive image. As Christians, we should be a reflection of Jesus.

Philippians 2:5 says, *"Let this mind be in you, which was also in Christ Jesus."* If you have the mind of Christ, your attitude will be good, and you'll learn how to be patient. Notice that I didn't say you would *automatically* be patient. I said you will *learn* how to be patient. We are all learning.

Your attitude will create an atmosphere that people around you will either love or despise. We all know people that we just like to be around. And then there are other people who aren't as pleasant to be around. Sometimes the reason we don't enjoy being around those people is that they have a negative attitude emanating from them. They don't even have to say a word.

If you need help with your attitude, pray this prayer from your heart: "Heavenly Father, help me work on my attitude. Help me to be alert in following You and Your Word. Help me keep my attitude, my thoughts, and my words in line with Your Word so that I emanate the love, joy, peace, and mercy of Jesus. I thank You for it in Jesus' Name, amen."

Chapter 8

Expect the Best

Whether you think you can or think you can't—you are right.

Henry Ford

⊷ ⊱⊰ ⊶

I t may be human nature to expect the worst, but if we're going to successfully take the future by storm, we must learn to expect the best.

Many godly people in the Bible expected the worst at one time or another in their lives. The first one I want to look at is David.

First Samuel chapter 27 relates part of the ongoing battle between King Saul and David. In chapter 26, we read that David spared Saul's life for the second time. David had the opportunity to kill Saul on more than one occasion, but he didn't because he knew Saul was the Lord's anointed. In this instance, David went into the cave where Saul was sleeping and took Saul's spear and water jug so that when Saul awoke, he would know that David had been there but had spared his life.

When Saul realized what David had done, he cried out to David, *". . . I have sinned: return, my son David: for I will no more do thee harm, because my soul was precious in thine eyes this day: behold, I have played the fool, and have erred exceedingly"* (1 Sam. 26:21). Then Saul blessed David, and David went on his way.

David and Saul had a running battle going for many years after David killed the giant Goliath. But after David spared Saul's life a second time, it seems they agreed to some sort of truce.

David trusted God throughout his battle with Saul, and God preserved him. But in First Samuel chapter 27, David had a lapse in faith.

1 SAMUEL 27:1

1   And DAVID SAID IN HIS HEART, I SHALL NOW PERISH ONE DAY BY THE HAND OF SAUL: there is nothing better for me than that I should speedily escape into the land of the Philistines; and Saul shall despair of me, to seek me any more in any coast of Israel: so shall I escape out of his hand.

Because David expected the worst to happen, he arose and went to live in the land of the Philistines, where he lived for some time.

Many times when we expect the worst, we are tormented by thoughts and images of what we think will happen. Yet most of the time, the things we expect never actually materialize.

David lost sight of the protecting power of God and began to focus on the circumstances. That caused David to change his expectations. After David lost sight of the fact that God had been protecting him all along, he began to expect to be destroyed by the hand of Saul.

God had taken care of David many times—delivering him from the lion and bear, from the sword of Goliath, and even from the hand of Saul. But in a moment of weakness, David lost his faith and went to dwell in the land of the Philistines, the enemy of his people.

Daniel and the Lion's Den

Now let's look at an example of someone who faced impossible odds, but because of his faith in God, he expected the best and triumphed. This is the story of Daniel and the lion's den.

In Daniel chapter 6, the would-be great prophet Daniel was still a young man who had just been taken into captivity. As was his custom, Daniel went to his window three times a day to pray to the Lord. His enemies hated him because they were jealous of his favor with the king. So they persuaded King Darius to sign a decree that said whoever prayed to any god or man other than the king in the next thirty days would be thrown into the lion's den. King Darius signed the decree, not knowing that the men were trying to trap Daniel.

The men waited until Daniel began to pray, and then they went to the king and reminded him of his decree. When the king heard that it was Daniel who was praying to God, he realized he had made a mistake, but there was nothing he could do to reverse the decree.

When Darius had Daniel thrown in the lion's den, he said to him, "May the God you serve protect you" (Dan. 6:16). And the next morning everyone, including the king, discovered that that's exactly what God did!

Two Men's Faith in Contrast

I want to contrast King Darius and Daniel to show that while one man expected the worst to happen, the other man expected the best and was mightily delivered.

King Darius had the authority to throw Daniel in the lion's den, and, although he didn't want to, Darius had to do it because he had decreed it. It was law, and even the king himself could not change it. After he put Daniel in the lion's den, Darius returned home for the night.

DANIEL 6:18 (*NIV*)

18 Then the king returned to his palace and spent the night without eating and without any entertainment being brought to him. And he could not sleep.

Darius couldn't sleep because he was concerned and worried about Daniel.

On the other hand, Daniel had a good night's sleep. I can imagine Daniel herded all of those lions together, used one of them for a pillow, and had the others lie down next to him to keep him warm through the night!

DANIEL 6:19-22 (*NIV*)
19 **At the first light of dawn, the king got up and hurried to the lions' den.**
20 **When he came near the den, he called to Daniel in an anguished voice, "Daniel, servant of the living God, has your God, whom you serve continually, been able to rescue you from the lions?"**
21 **Daniel answered, "O king, live for ever!**
22 **My God sent his angel, and he shut the mouths of the lions. They have not hurt me, because I was found innocent in his sight. Nor have I ever done any wrong before you, O king."**

Because Daniel trusted in God and expected the best, he was able to tell the king, "Never fear, O King. I'm here, and everything's fine. My God has taken care of me."

You see, one man was expecting the worst, and the other one was living by faith. Faith rests; unbelief wallows in restlessness. When you are expecting the worst, you will toss and turn all night. But when you expect the best, you will rest in the peace of God.

Think Positive Thoughts

You may be saying, "What do these stories have to do with me today?"

Plenty. For example, if you stand strong in faith for thirty days and then step out of faith, that one lapse could nullify thirty days of believing God. The devil knows that, so he is ever trying to get you out of faith.

When you are standing in faith for something, you cannot afford to think negative thoughts. When you hear news of things that are happening around the world or in your city, you cannot afford to think in the area of the negative. You have to always anticipate that God will take care of you.

It's nearly impossible to read a newspaper or watch television news commentaries without your natural mind immediately wanting to anticipate the worst. But if we want our faith in God and His Word to work, we cannot afford to allow the pressures of this world that constantly bombard our ears, eyes, and mind to affect us in the least.

I'm not saying that we're not to act in a reasonable fashion. We should always use common sense. I am talking about learning how to believe God and anticipate that what God says in His Word concerning you will come to pass.

God Is Still God

God said that He would supply our needs (Phil. 4:19). You may ask, "How?" I don't know. It's not my responsibility or yours to know how. Our only responsibility is to believe God and take Him at His Word.

God's Word says He will meet our needs. The way He meets our needs is His business. Our business is to take God at His Word and allow His Word to be the final authority.

Someone might say, "But aren't you concerned about inflation? What if the price of fuel goes up again? What if the tax structure changes?"

Well, if I listened to everything on the news, I would begin to get in despair and anticipate the worst. But I listen to the truth of God's Word. And no matter what happens, I'm going to do what the Bible says, because the Word of God says that whatever I believe—whatever I have faith in the Word for—will come to pass.

Things in this world may change, but God is still the same (Heb. 13:8). God and the Word are the only things that don't change. And God said in His Word that He would meet all of my needs (Phil. 4:19). Most of the time, God meets my needs through dollar bills. But my trust is not in the dollar bill. My trust for security is not in my job. My trust for security in life is based on God and His Word. Matthew 24:35 says, *"Heaven and earth shall pass away, but my words shall not pass away."* If God said it, I believe it. And that settles it.

Let the Word Have First Place

In Mark chapter 16, we read about three women who expected the worst, only to discover that what they were anticipating never took place.

MARK 16:1–4 (*NIV*)
1   **When the Sabbath was over, Mary Magdalene, Mary the mother of James, and Salome bought spices so that they might go to anoint Jesus' body.**
2   **Very early on the first day of the week, just after sunrise, they were on their way to the tomb**
3   **and they asked each other, "Who will roll the stone away from the entrance of the tomb?"**
4   **But when they looked up, they saw that the stone, which was very large, had been rolled away.**

These women became bothered because they were expecting the worst. Before they even reached the tomb, they worried, "Who's going to roll the stone away?" But when they got there, they discovered that it wasn't even an issue, because the stone had already been rolled away.

You may have been worrying about all sorts of things. But if you will just follow God and His path for your life, you'll find that when you get to where you're going, everything will already be taken care of. But if you spend all your time worrying and wondering what's going to happen in the future, you will live a life of torment. Remember that if you could fix your situation on your own, you would have already done so. Now it's time to just lean on the Word of God and walk on.

Sometimes we allow the enemy to play with our minds rather than allowing the Word to have first place. Once again, let me say that I'm not telling you to act unwisely. I'm telling you that if you know how to believe God and stand your ground, you will let the Word of God be the first and final word in your life.

You Can Do All Things Through Jesus Christ

Someone once said to me, "It sounds like you don't know how to take 'no' for an answer."

I answered, "Well, I don't believe in the phrase, 'It can't be done.' "

I always expect the best because I believe God can make a way where there is no way. Anything is possible when you have faith in the Word of God. Philippians 4:13 says we can do *all* things through Christ who strengthens us.

Many people haven't gotten hold of that scripture yet. They read it, but they haven't got hold of it. It says, "I *can.*" There is no "can't" involved. It's "I *can.*" Can do what? *All* things. Not *some* things—*all* things. How can we do all things? Through Jesus Christ!

I can do whatever needs to be done, because I'm in Christ. It's not because of who *I* am, but because of who *Jesus* is and because I'm in Him.

Some people think that this verse only applies to spiritual things. But Paul wasn't just talking about spiritual things; he is talking about natural things too. Notice it says, *"I can do ALL THINGS through Christ which strengtheneth me."* That means that I can do whatever I need to do in the way of spiritual things *and* in the way of natural things.

Someone might say, "Wait a minute. If you keep talking that way, you're going to pump people up too much, and they're going to become egotistical and conceited."

No, it's not conceit when you say, "I can do it *through Jesus Christ.*" We may be doing the physical work, but it's Christ Who is giving us the strength and power.

The Prophet Elijah

There is nothing you can't go through successfully—there is nothing you can't handle—if you stay in Christ. The problem is, many Christians get into difficulty and remove themselves from His peace and protection by getting into fear and expecting the worst to happen.

Elijah, the great prophet of God, is a good example of what I'm talking about. The Bible tells us that Elijah did many great exploits for God. In First Kings chapter 18, we read how Elijah defeated all the prophets of Baal. But in chapter 19, it's Elijah who acts defeated.

1 KINGS 19:1–4 (*NIV*)

1   Now Ahab told Jezebel everything Elijah had done and how he had killed all the prophets with the sword.

2   So Jezebel sent a messenger to Elijah to say, "May the gods deal with me, be it ever so severely, if by this time tomorrow I do not make your life like that of one of them."

3   Elijah was afraid and ran for his life. When he came to Beersheba in Judah, he left his servant there,

4   while he himself went a day's journey into the desert. He came to a broom tree, sat down under it and prayed that he might die. "I have had enough, Lord," he said. "Take my life; I am no better than my ancestors."

Let's picture this for a moment. Here is the great man of God, Elijah, who was just on the mountain where fire came down from Heaven and consumed a sacrifice that had been soaked with twelve barrels of water. Elijah, the man who had just killed all the prophets of Baal, turned and ran away in fear for his life because the queen said she was going to cut his head off for killing her prophets!

This scenario reminds me of some Christians. They win a tremendous victory in which God blesses them abundantly. Then the devil hits them with something insignificant by comparison, and they start running scared, saying, "What are we going to do now?"

In First Kings 19:4, Elijah so expected the worst that he didn't want to live anymore. He said, "Lord, it's no use for me to live any more. Just take my life." Elijah didn't really want to die. If that were the case, he wouldn't have run away. If he had really wanted to die, he could have stayed where he was, and Jezebel would have quickly obliged him! No, he was having a lapse of faith because he heard some bad news and expected the worst.

Elijah didn't need to run away when Jezebel threatened to kill him. He could have stayed where he was, depended on the power of God, and survived. Elijah knew how to call on God in times of trouble. He had just proved the power of God on the mount (see First Kings 18:19–40). And if Elijah had stayed where he was and continued to believe God, God would have delivered him again.

When Jezebel's men came to execute Elijah, what if Elijah had called on the Lord Jehovah the way he did on the mountain? What if he raised his head toward Heaven and said, "Lord Jehovah, the God of Abraham, Isaac, and Jacob, I call upon You now for protecting power"? Guess whose heads would have been rolling? Not the prophet's head, but the heads of the people who were coming against him!

But instead, Elijah lost his faith. This incident shows that just because you had a victory yesterday is no guarantee that you're going to automatically have the victory tomorrow. You must keep yourself spiritually fit and make the decision every day to believe God's Word above all else.

The Apostle Paul

In Acts chapter 27, we read that the Apostle Paul was on a ship that had been caught in a severe storm. The ship had been pitching and rolling for several days. The crew threw everything overboard, yet the boat was still about to go under. The entire crew feared for their lives, except for Paul, who stood on the deck of the ship and said, ". . . keep up your courage, men, for I have faith in God that it will happen just as he told me" (Acts 27:25 *NIV*).

Why was Paul so confident? Because an angel of God had appeared to him during the night to reassure him that he would live to stand before Caesar. Not only did the angel tell Paul that he would live through the storm, but he also said that those who sailed with Paul would survive (Acts 27:22–24). And Paul believed and acted upon the words of the angel of God!

Can you stand on the deck of your boat, so to speak, while you are being tossed to and fro in the storms of life, and say, "I have faith in God that things will happen just as He has told me"? That is the place you must get to in Him and the expectation you must have.

You can't afford to say, "Who's going to roll the stone away?" Or "I need to run for my life!" No, faith anticipates the victory! So begin to expect the best and talk the best. Don't talk about what you don't have; talk about what you *do* have. Talk about who you are and what you have in Christ.

Don't sit around talking negative. If you allow your ears to become garbage cans, always listening to junk, you'll start talking junk. But if you always listen to the Word of God, you will talk the Word.

You become like those with whom you hang around. And you become what you hear. The reason so many homes are in peril today is because people sit around watching and listening to junk on TV. If you allow a negative seed to be planted in your heart, the devil will try to bring that seed to fruition.

You can't help what is being aired on the television channels, but you *can* change the channel on *your* television! You might say, "What does what I watch on TV have to do with what you're talking about?" When you feed on junk, it will steal the Word of God from your heart. It will keep you from living for God, and you'll begin to expect the worst. Your faith will not be strong enough to expect the best.

The Simple Approach

Keep your faith strong and stop anticipating the worst. Begin to claim what the Word says is yours by saying, "I can do all things through Christ which strengthens me."

It doesn't matter what anyone else says is going to happen in the future. God's Word says that He will take care of you. Even if inflation goes "sky high," God's Word still works.

God took care of the Israelites as they wandered around in the desert, and He will take care of you too. Even if He has to rain down manna in your front yard! God did it for His children in the Old Testament, and if He needs to, He will do it for His children today!

My trust is in God's Word. It doesn't matter what comes or goes, who's in or out of office, what political party is ruling or not ruling—God's Word will work.

Someone might say, "That is a very simple approach."

Well, Jesus said that's the kind of approach we're supposed to have. In Mark 10:15 Jesus said, *"Verily I say unto you, Whosoever shall not receive the kingdom of God as a little child, he shall not enter therein."*

When you tell a little child something, he believes you. He doesn't go worrying about what you said, and he doesn't keep coming back and asking you if it's going to happen. He expects it to be just as you told him.

Let us be same way with God. If God said He would do something, then expect Him to do it. Expect it to be done, not because of who you are, but because of who you are in Christ Jesus.

You don't ever have to anticipate the worst or have a lapse of faith again, but you will if you feed on junk instead of on the truth of God's Word. You can't get the victory with just head knowledge or by simply wishing it's going to happen. You have to expect it and believe it in your heart. You have the victory when you believe God's Word no matter what comes or goes—no matter what you feel, see, taste, touch, or smell.

Chapter 9

What Comes Out When The Pressure Is On?

My worth to God in public is what I am in private.

Oswald Chambers

A s I talk about taking the future by storm, I'm not going to
pretend that it's always an easy thing to do. The pressures
of life come to everyone. The important thing is how we
respond to the different pressures we face. Whatever is on the
inside of us will comes out when the pressure is on, so what we
put in is vital.

What sort of influence is guiding your life? We've all heard
maxims such as these: "The quickest way to double your
money is to fold it over and put it back in your pocket,"
"Letting the cat out of the bag is a whole lot easier than putting it back in," and "If you find yourself in a hole, the first
thing you need to do is stop digging." Some mottos or "words
to live by" may be humorous, but many of them offer good
advice.

We all have maxims or mottos upon which we base our
life. Throughout the years, many different things have been
said to all of us. They may be sayings or phrases that we
learned while growing up or while going to school.

Miss Fowler, my first grade teacher, told me something years ago when I was her student that I still live by today. She said, "The word 'can't' doesn't exist unless you allow it to." Miss Fowler taught me that saying something "can't be done" is the only thing that keeps me from getting it done. To this day, I don't say I can't do something.

Also, everything I do, I do with one hundred percent effort because of something my father told me when I was growing up. He always said, "Son, if something is worth doing, then it's worth doing right and it's worth doing with everything you've got—and more too. If you aren't going to do something with everything you have, then don't do it at all."

I took my father's advice to heart, and that philosophy has become my way of life. I give everything I have in everything I do. I am convinced that if something is worth doing, then it's worth doing with everything I've got or I won't do it at all.

Some people just go through the motions, so to speak. Those people never accomplish anything; they're just here. But the Bible wants us to be more than just here! God tells us in His holy Word that He wants us to *be something* and to *do something*.

What Goes in Is What Comes Out

I have two children who can tell you that if they've heard me say this one time, they've heard me say it a thousand times: "You and God together can accomplish anything."

Every day when Craig and Denise got out of the car to go to school, I told them, "God loves you and Daddy loves you. Have a great day." Every night when I tucked them in bed, even before they could talk, I would tell them, "You are a success. And with God on your side, you can be whatever you want to be and you can do whatever you want to do."

I'm happy to say that today both my children have graduated from college and RHEMA Bible Training Center and are serving God in full-time ministry.

Why is it that some people grow up to become strong individuals who conquer life? It may be due to what was instilled in them by their parents. Maybe as children they were always told that they can and will succeed in life.

Well, once a person starts to believe he can be someone and do something in life, then he really can! The problem is that many people have been told the wrong thing—and they began to believe it. So their lives reflect their wrong thinking.

Maybe they were told that they were nothing, that they weren't worth anything, or that they'd never be a success in life. So what did they do? They acted out those expectations because that's what had been put in them.

As the saying goes, *What goes IN is what comes OUT!* Take a look at a sponge. If you put a sponge in clear water and then squeeze it, clear water comes out. But if you take that same sponge and wipe up a bunch of oil and grease and then squeeze it, dirty-looking junk will come out. Why? Because that's what went into it!

Whatever goes into you is what will come out of you when you're under pressure. If your life is filled with gossip, pornography, drunkenness, drug abuse, anger, pettiness, and negative things that tear down rather than build up, when you start getting "squeezed" by the pressures of life—nothing but garbage will come out.

But if your life is filled with love, mercy, forgiveness, the Word of God, prayer, songs of praise and worship, and the grace of God, when the pressures of life come and you're squeezed—out will come love, mercy, grace, and so forth.

Build Upon God's Word

We have built our lives on all sorts of maxims and sayings, but we should also have Scripture that guides and directs our lives. Because whatever is written on your mind and heart will control your life, it's important that you build your life upon what the Word of God says.

95

Hebrews 10:16 tells us that God has made a covenant with us concerning this very thing.

HEBREWS 10:16 (*NIV*)

16 This is the covenant I will make with them after that time, says the Lord, I will put my laws in their hearts, and I will write them on their minds.

If you will study God's Word, He will put His laws into your heart. And Jesus said, "If you remain in me and my words remain in you, ask whatever you wish, and it will be given you" (John 15:7 *NIV*). Well, how are His words going to remain in you unless you put them there in the first place!

Cow Sense

We must be concerned about what we're putting inside our heart. We need to be careful who and what we listen to. If we listen long enough to what is contrary to God's Word and follow after it, we're going to get in a mess.

You need to understand that what you take in is what you're going to put out! When the pressures of life come, you're either going to put out God's Word ("Thank God, all my needs are met according to His riches in glory," "By His stripes I'm healed," and so forth), or you're going to say, "Oh, my Lord, why did you let this happen to me?" It just depends on what you've been looking at and who you've been listening to.

No matter who we listen to or what we read, we must have enough discernment to know if the teaching is in line with God's Word or it is off a little bit. I remember a certain traveling minister who was teaching tremendous things on prayer, but got overboard in another area. You see, people can get off course in one area and still be on course in other areas. That is why we have to have enough discernment to "eat the hay and spit out the sticks." If you've ever fed cattle, you know what I mean by that.

I haven't bailed hay in years, but I remember that we put bailing wire around the hay to form bales and then put the bales into stacks. But as the baler went down the field picking up hay, it also picked up rocks, cans, and anything else that was on the ground. All of the junk got bailed with the hay.

But if you go out in the field after the cows have finished eating the hay that was bailed, only the hay is gone. All the junk—the rocks, cans, sticks, and so forth—is left untouched. You have to rake up all the junk. Cows are smart enough to eat the hay and leave the junk alone!

Unfortunately, some Christians aren't as smart as the cows. No matter what teaching is put before them, they take it and digest it—whether it's good for them or not! They're like the little baby birds sitting in the nest waiting for the mama bird to bring them food. No matter what the mother brings, the babies just open their mouths and swallow. We need to have more discretion than that!

Feed Your Faith

You see, we need to realize that just because a certain individual says something doesn't necessarily make it so! Even the Apostle Paul said, "If I or an angel or an emissary come or someone else comes preaching anything else than what I've already told you, count it accursed (Gal. 1:8).

We need to be careful what we take in because what goes in is what's going to come out when the pressure is on. It's so important that we read our Bible and know what God's Word says. God's Word feeds our hearts and minds.

Romans 10:17 says that faith comes by hearing and hearing by the Word of God. When you feed yourself on God's Word, you are feeding your faith. Then when the pressures of life come, and life begins to squeeze you, faith and courage will come out. You will have the courage to face any situation that comes along because you have faith to believe that God will take you through anything and everything!

Again, Hebrews 10:16 says, "This is the covenant I will make with them after that time, says the Lord. I will put my laws in their hearts, and I will write them on their minds" (*NIV*). God puts the laws in our hearts and minds when we read or hear the Word.

And when we get God's Word in our hearts, it becomes part of our minds—our thinking. Then when we are squeezed, out comes love. When someone does us wrong, out comes forgiveness. When someone else has made a mistake or falls short, out comes grace and mercy.

A Fight for Keeps

We need to understand that we are in a fight—the fight of faith—and that this is a fight for keeps. We have to make an effort to keep God's Word in our heart and mind. The Bible says that you should guard your heart, for out of it flow the issues of life (Prov. 4:23).

The devil will try any way he can to steal the Word from you or to keep it from producing in your life. Sometimes the devil uses offenses or resentments to keep Christians from receiving what God has for them.

Many Christians have allowed some deep hurt or gross injustice to keep them from receiving God's best. They have allowed their wound to keep them from being a blessing to others, and now the devil has them exactly where he wants them. They are no good to themselves, no good to anyone else, and no good to the Kingdom of God.

If the devil can't entice you to sin, he will do other things to hinder you. He might say, "Remember what So-and-so did to you? You ought to tell everyone what kind of person he really is . . . ."

When you start dwelling on what other people have done, the devil has you off course. Once again, you have to know what the Word says so that when the pressure comes, God's Word is what comes out. The Bible says we are to pray for those who hurt us and forgive them (Matt. 5:44). And the Word also says to restore those who have fallen in a spirit of meekness lest we fall ourselves (Gal. 6:1).

Forget the Past

I've heard so many people talk about how they've been rejected. They say, "I've been rejected all my life. I've been so deeply hurt."

You can choose to dwell on the hurtful things that others have done or said until you become a sponge that's "full of nothing." But when the pressures of life come, you'll only hinder yourself and others. Or you can hide God's words inside your heart until they become a part of your mind as well. And when someone does you wrong, love and forgiveness come out of you. When someone has made a mistake, grace and mercy come out of you!

I have determined to walk in love no matter what anyone says about me. I've made up my mind to simply say, "Lord, You know my heart. You know how I live, and You know what I believe. Forgive them, Lord, for what they've said and done. Now I'm going on with You."

No matter what other people say or do, your future and quality of life depend on what *you* say and do.

You see, it all comes back to having the laws of God in your heart and in your mind. I am assured by God that it makes no difference what happened in the past because Hebrews 10:17 says that God doesn't remember our sins and lawless acts anymore. If you have asked for forgiveness for whatever you might have done, then forget about it! God has!

Why wallow in the past? Many people wallow in past hurts because they want acceptance. But God Almighty has already accepted you!

Circle 'Yes' or 'No'

We can all remember the notes we passed to our friends when we were in grade school. Up until about the fourth grade, boys and girls didn't want to have anything to do with each other. But in the fifth or sixth grade, we all begin to write little notes, saying "I like you. Do you like me? Circle: Yes, No, Maybe." We weren't looking for love. We might call it "puppy love," but, really, we were looking for acceptance from some-one we liked.

I want to tell you something: We have the best note that's ever been written. God wrote us a note called the Bible, and in it He said, "*Yes*, I like you." He went a step further and wrote, "*Yes*, you are loved. *Yes*, you are forgiven. *Yes*, you are a child of God. *Yes*, you're my friend. *Yes*, I am your Heavenly Father. *Yes*, you are a child of the King."

Now we can approach the Throne of God with confidence! Why? Because Jesus said, "*Yes*, you're free from sin. *Yes*, you're free from guilt. *Yes*, you're free from hurt. *Yes*, you're free from any abuse that's ever been done to you."

Jesus Christ is the "yes" written in our hearts and in our minds. God has sent us a great love note. And He said in this love note, "I will never leave you or forsake you (Heb. 13:5). I will supply all of your needs (Phil. 4:19). I will heal your body (1 Peter 2:24).

You don't have to walk through life alone. God has accepted you. It doesn't matter where you are—you could be by yourself in the middle of the desert, but you are not alone!

It's Up to You

What happens in your life is up to you. God has given you all the answers. You can walk through life hurt and cowed down if you want to. But I'm going to hold my head up, and I'm going to walk through life with Jesus Christ as my power and strength. I'm going to walk through the trials and tribula-tions and come out on the other side with a smile on my face, a dance in my step, and a song in my heart. You can do the same by hiding God's Word in your heart.

Just remember this: Jesus is "Yes"! *Yes*, He loves you. *Yes*, He cares about you. If you start feeling hurt or rejected, remem-ber that Jesus is with you. He hasn't rejected you, and He never will. He's putting His arm around you and saying, "Come on, let's go. You can overcome."

Make a decision today to hide God's Word in your heart and become a sponge that is full of His Word and His power. Then when the pressures of life begin to squeeze you, no matter what anyone else says or does, nothing's going to come out of you except courage, love, faith, and power!

Chapter 10

Facing the Fire

Victory at all costs, victory in spite of all terror,
victory however long and hard the road may be.

Winston Churchill

────◄◄►►────

We're talking about taking our future by storm. The only way we will be able to do that—the only way we will find success in life—is by adopting an attitude that says, "I cannot be defeated, and I will not quit!"

Unfortunately, some people think that when they have that kind of attitude, they will then "float through life on flowery beds of ease." It doesn't work that way. Although some people don't like to hear this, no matter what kind of attitude we have, we will still face obstacles and opposition in life. Our attitude just determines whether or not we will have victory over the obstacles.

I don't want you to think that you won't ever face the fire. I want you to know what to do when you're in the fire so that you will walk through it unharmed!

You *will* face obstacles in life, but you can overcome them by your faith and commitment to God. When you hold on to God's Word and believe Him in spite of every opposition, He will deliver you!

Standing Tall

In Daniel chapter 3, we read that when three young Hebrew men—Shadrach, Meshach, and Abednego—were taken into Babylonian captivity, they faced extreme pressure to abandon their faith in God.

King Nebuchadnezzar had an image of gold made, and then he gathered all the officials and rulers of the provinces in his kingdom to come to the dedication of the image. Then the king issued a decree that when the people heard the music, they were to fall down and worship the image.

But Shadrach, Meshach, and Abednego had purposed in their hearts to serve and obey the one true God—at any cost.

DANIEL 3:1–6

1   **Nebuchadnezzar the king made an image of gold, whose height was threescore cubits** [about 90 feet], **and the breadth thereof six cubits: he set it up in the plain of Dura, in the province of Babylon.**

2   **Then Nebuchadnezzar the king sent to gather together the princes, the governors, and the captains, the judges, the treasurers, the counsellors, the sheriffs, and all the rulers of the provinces, to come to the dedication of the image which Nebuchadnezzar the king had set up.**

3   **Then the princes, the governors, and captains, the judges, the treasurers, the counsellors, the sheriffs, and all the rulers of the provinces, were gathered together unto the dedication of the image that Nebuchadnezzar the king had set up; and they stood before the image that Nebuchadnezzar had set up.**

4   **Then an herald cried aloud, To you it is commanded, O people, nations, and languages,**

5   **That at what time ye hear the sound of the cornet, flute, harp, sackbut, psaltery, dulcimer, and all kinds of musick, ye fall down and worship the golden image that Nebuchadnezzar the king hath set up:**

6 **And whoso falleth not down and worshippeth shall
the same hour be cast into the midst of a burning fiery
furnace.**

Well, when the music was played, all the people fell down
and worshipped the golden image—everyone that is, except the
three young Hebrew men. Then certain Chaldeans went to
Nebuchadnezzar and said, "King, you made a decree that all the
people should fall down and worship the image, did you not?"

He answered in the positive, and they said, "Well, there are
certain Jews whom you have set over your affairs, Shadrach,
Meshach, and Abednego, who did not regard you, O King.
They did not worship the golden image, and they did not serve
your god." (Part of the problem was that the Chaldeans were
disgruntled because outsiders had been set over them.) So
Nebuchadnezzar, in a rage of fury, said, "Bring those three guys
to me" (Dan. 3:7–13)!

DANIEL 3:14–15

14 **Nebuchadnezzar spake and said unto them, Is it true,
O Shadrach, Meshach, and Abednego, do not ye serve
my gods, nor worship the golden image which I have
set up?**

15 **Now if ye be ready** [or if you're ready to do] **that at
what time ye hear the sound of the cornet, flute, harp,
sackbut, psaltery, and dulcimer, and all kinds of
musick, ye fall down and worship the image which I
have made; well: but if ye worship not, ye shall be cast
the same hour into the midst of a burning fiery furnace; and who is that God that shall deliver you out of
my hands?**

I want you to notice that not only did Nebuchadnezzar
challenge these three young men, but he challenged Almighty
God! He said, "Who is this God that shall deliver you out of
my hands?" That is almost the attitude of the world today
when you start talking about the God of deliverance and

power. It may not be in spoken words as we have here, but that seems to be the attitude of many people.

Yet Shadrach, Meshach, and Abednego didn't care what the rest of the world was doing or saying. They chose to obey God!

DANIEL 3:16–18

16 Shadrach, Meshach, and Abednego, answered and said to the king, O Nebuchadnezzar, we are not careful to answer thee in this matter.

17 If it be so, our God whom we serve is able to deliver us from the burning fiery furnace, and he will deliver us out of thine hand, O king.

18 But if not, BE IT KNOWN UNTO THEE, O king, that WE WILL NOT SERVE THY GODS, nor worship the golden image which thou hast set up.

Those three young Hebrew men said, "We don't even have to think about it. We know *where we are*; we know *who we are*; and we know *where we're going*. But we're still not going to bow down to your god!"

Are You in the Fire?

You may feel as though you're facing the fire today, or you may feel as though you're already in the furnace, because of the things the enemy has brought against you. I realize that you're probably never going to face a real fiery furnace, but the circumstances of life–trials and tribulations–may seem like a fiery furnace to you! So you need to learn how to face the fire. When everyone else has crumbled and compromised under the pressure, you must stand strong!

Can you imagine what strong faith and determination it took for those three young men to stand strong for God? There were other Jewish people in Babylon with them. Everyone else had bowed down to the image. The others had been taught, just as Shadrach, Meshach, and Abednego had, that they should have no other god before the Lord (Exod. 20:3). But they were in a strange land and they compromised. They lost their faith and commitment.

Yet here were three young men, probably in their late teens or early twenties, who made a decision to face the fire rather than compromise. It takes boldness to stand when everyone else is going in the other direction.

Never Compromise

Young people, I know that it's not easy to stand for what you believe when all of your peers are pulling on you and pressure is against you. But that's when you learn to grow up with God. That's when you learn how to become a man or woman of God, or a wimp for the devil.

Teenagers, there are many adults who have already gone down that trail. They can tell you that it may look good, but it's a trail of sorrow. It's a trail that will lead you to nowhere!

The crowd might say, "Oh, it won't hurt. Just come on and go over here with us."

Yes, it will hurt. Many times many people think, *Well, I'm going to help them.* You can't help sinners by going where they're going or doing what they're doing. You help them by standing your ground and saying, "I'm not going to do that."

I thank God that during my high school years when my friends were going to do something they shouldn't, I had enough courage to say, "Stop the car and let me out!" Then I walked home. My mind would say, "Oh, just go along. You don't have to participate." But for me, just being there would have been a compromise.

You must understand that if you decide not to compromise, you're going to face the fire. For Shadrach, Meshach, and Abednego, that meant facing a death decree. To not bow down to the golden image meant the fiery furnace—death! But these young men knew what the Word said. They had been taught the Law as every other young Hebrew man had. They knew what it said about not having any other god before the Lord, and they chose to follow God (Exod. 20:3; Isa. 45:6).

Now they were in a foreign place, and maybe no one would ever have known that they bowed down to the golden image, but God would have known. You may think you're fooling everyone, but God knows! God knows everything. No one else may know, but God does.

I'm sure their minds tried to convince them, *Oh, it won't hurt to bow down just this once to escape the fiery furnace.* Yes, it will! If you sin once, it's easier to sin twice. If you do it twice, it's easier to do it three times. If you do it four times, you can forget it!

Sometimes You Need to Be Selfish

Shadrach, Meshach, and Abednego had buddies there in Babylon, but they didn't care what their buddies did or said! That's something you need to understand: When it comes to your spiritual life, you need to become selfish.

When it comes to helping others and giving and so forth, you should not be selfish. But when it comes to your personal spiritual life, you need to become selfish. Don't misunderstand what I'm saying. I want you to take it the right way. Don't go around saying that I said it's fine to be selfish, because I didn't. What I mean is, your spiritual life is *your* responsibility.

You see, having a relationship with God is not a family proposition or a corporate thing. It's a personal thing, one-on-one. Mama can't do it for you; Daddy can't do it for you; neither can your husband or wife or some preacher. No one else can do it for you. *You* have to take care of your relationship with God yourself!

And when you really know who you are in Christ, and your faith in Him is strong, you won't turn back. Strong faith doesn't compromise or quit under pressure. Strong faith tenaciously holds on to the things of God—even when it looks as if it's no use! Strong faith will not give up in the face of utter defeat. That's how you face the fire. That's the way you become a success with God.

Don't Bow Under Pressure

Shadrach, Meshach, and Abednego refused to bow to the pressure. In the biggest test of their lives, they made a decision to stand for God—even if it meant death. Later we'll see how God rewarded them because of their strong stand for Him. But first, let's look at Daniel 3:17 and 18 again. These verses have been kicked and battered about because they seem to be contradictory statements.

DANIEL 3:17–18

17 **If it be so, our GOD whom we serve IS ABLE TO DELIVER US from the burning fiery furnace, and he will deliver us out of thine hand, O king.**

18 **BUT IF NOT, be it known unto thee, O king, that WE WILL NOT SERVE THY GODS, nor worship the golden image which thou hast set up.**

Now on the surface, without really thinking about it, it does look like these verses contradict each other. But if you'll look at them in the light of understanding *strong faith*, you'll begin to see that they don't contradict each other at all.

Verse 17 is Shadrach, Meshach, and Abednego's faith talking: "Our God is able to deliver us." Verse 18 shows their commitment to their faith: "We will stand by what we believe, no matter what!" If you realize that verse 17 is a statement of faith, and verse 18 demonstrates the commitment that keeps faith strong, you have no trouble understanding these scriptures.

If you're going to take a stand for God and receive whatever it is you need from Him, not only must you have strong faith and make a confession of your faith, but you must also be committed to backing up your faith.

That's where most people fail. They understand faith and how to live by faith, and they can quote the Word to you. But their commitment to their faith is where they're falling down. They're not committed to standing when they come under fire.

Instead they begin to compromise. They begin to pull back and ask, "Why?" Friends, ours is not to ask why. Ours is to say as the Apostle Paul said on the deck of that ship in the midst of a storm: *". . . I believe God, that it shall be even as it was told me"* (Acts 27:25). That was his statement, period.

Let me tell you a little secret: We're going to face all kinds of trials and situations. But if we will hold fast our confession of faith, God will deliver us out of them all. It depends on what *we* do.

In Daniel 3:17 and 18, those young Hebrew men were saying, "No matter what happens, we're still committed to our faith in God." People today don't like commitments, because commitment demands responsibility. They won't stand up to their friends and say, "God doesn't do those things, and I'm a child of God. And the Bible tells me to mirror my Father, so I don't do those things." Instead they cop out, saying, "My church doesn't believe in that," so they don't have to take any responsibility.

You have to stand up for what *you* believe. People may look at you funny and call you every name they can think of. Just remember, in the end, they're the ones who are going to burn and you're the one who is going to glow. Don't worry about the fiery tests you face down here on earth. You have to learn how to come through the fiery tests on earth so you won't end up in the fires of hell!

The Fourth Man

When Shadrach, Meshach, and Abednego stood up for what they believed, they were tied up and thrown into the fiery furnace (Dan. 3:19–22). But God delivered them!

DANIEL 3:23–25

23 And these three men, Shadrach, Meshach, and Abednego, fell down bound into the midst of the burning fiery furnace.

24 Then Nebuchadnezzar the king was astonied, and rose

up in haste, and spake, and said unto his counsellors,
Did not we cast three men bound into the midst of the
fire? They answered and said unto the king, True, O king.

25 He answered and said, Lo, I see four men loose, walking in the midst of the fire, and they have no hurt; and
the form of the fourth is like the Son of God.

I want you to notice that verse 23 says "... *Shadrach,
Meshach, and Abednego, FELL DOWN BOUND into the midst of
the burning fiery furnace.*" That means they were bound, hand
and foot. They went into the fire bound, but they were quickly
loosed. In astonishment, the king jumped up and asked, "Hey,
didn't we throw three guys in there bound?"

The king's servants replied, "Yes, we did."

Then the king said, "I see four men loose, walking around
in the fire, and there is no hurt on them! [In other words,
they're not burning.] And the fourth man with them looks like
the Son of God."

You may go into a fiery furnace bound, but look around,
and you'll see that you have been loosed! *And* the Son of God
is in there walking with you, and there's no hurt on you!

Well, Nebuchadnezzar called Shadrach, Meshach, and
Abednego out of the furnace, and when they walked out, all
those governors, princes, and everyone else saw that the fire
didn't have any power over them (v. 27).

Our Fire Suit

Friend, I want to tell you something: You have a fire suit—
it's the power and anointing of God. The circumstances of life
may bind you up and throw you into the fire, so to speak, but
you have a fire protection suit on!

Let me explain what I mean. I like car races, especially
NASCAR. Well, if you want to drive in a car race, you have to
abide by the safety rules, or they're not going to let you in the
race. First, you have to put on a special kind of sock and
undergarment, then you put a suit on top of that and put a

hood on your head; each piece is fire retardant. So race car drivers could be in a fire and still escape unburned because of the fire retardant suits that they wear.

Their fire retardant suits will only hold up for a short period of time—they're only designed to last long enough for a rescue. But the fire retardant suit that you and I have—the anointing and power of God—is a suit that lasts *forever*! And no fiery dart of the enemy can penetrate it!

You're not going to float through life without having a problem, test, or trial. You're going to face the fire, but if you have strong faith and strong commitment to the Word of God, you'll go into the fire and walk out with no hurt on you. And when you come out, everyone will recognize it, just as King Nebuchadnezzar did.

DANIEL 3:29

29 Therefore I [Nebuchadnezzar] **make a decree, That every people, nation, and language, which speak any thing amiss against the God of Shadrach, Meshach, and Abednego, shall be cut in pieces, and their houses shall be made a dunghill: because THERE IS NO OTHER GOD THAT CAN DELIVER AFTER THIS SORT.**

There's only one God! All the so-called gods are false, or they're the figment of someone's imagination. Those religious leaders have died and their bones are still in the grave, but the God of gods is alive and well! And He will see you through the fire; He will see you through the flood and whatever else you go through (Isa. 43:2)!

God will walk with us *in the fire*, and He will walk *out of the fire* with us. We must not compromise and lose our faith and commitment. We've come this far by faith! Let's not compromise and lose out now. Shadrach, Meshach, and Abednego walked out of the fire, because "there is no other God!"

Many people cry and complain when they face the fire, because they just have a so-called god. But you and I have that "no other God." We have El Shaddai, *the God who is more than enough*! We have the God of peace, righteousness, and everything that we need or want!

Deliverance and Promotion

Because Shadrach, Meshach, and Abednego refused to compromise their faith and commitment, not only did God deliver them from the fire, but they were promoted!

DANIEL 3:30

30 Then the king PROMOTED Shadrach, Meshach, and Abednego, in the province of Babylon.

God will do for you what He did for Shadrach, Meshach, and Abednego. When you live by faith and are totally sold out in your commitment to God, you will go into the fire bound and walk out loosed. And then there is nothing but promotion left for you!

If you feel as though you're in the fire right now, don't lose your faith or waver in your commitment to God. You will walk out of the fire unharmed, because there is no other god, but God!

Chapter 11

Keep Striking the Ground

I do the very best I know how—the very best I can;
and I mean to keep on doing so until the very end.
Abraham Lincoln

W e've learned that just because we have the attitude "I cannot be defeated, and I will not quit" doesn't mean we
won't ever have any obstacles in our life. We must simply learn
how to go over them to victory.

It's important to have a battle plan, so to speak, for what
to do when hard times come. When you are up against a problem, that's not the time to lie down and say, "Why is this happening to me? I'm a person of faith." No, that's the time to
stay in faith and keep moving.

We've all had to deal with disappointment in life. Sometimes
disappointment can lead to discouragement and depression.
These are three things we sometimes have to deal with as we
face the storms of life: *disappointment*, *discouragement*, and
depression. Notice that I said you will have to "deal with" these
things. There is a difference between dealing with something
and being in bondage to it. We may have to deal with these
things, but when we deal with them according to the Word of
God, we will always get the victory.

Disappointment can come with a career setback, a financial
reversal, or a broken relationship. The important thing is how

we deal with disappointment. When adversity comes, we must keep striking the ground.

The phrase "keep striking the ground" comes from a story in Second Kings chapter 2. Joash, king of Israel, was discouraged and depressed at the prospect of a Syrian invasion, so he went to get advice from the prophet Elisha.

2 KINGS 13:14

14 Now Elisha was fallen sick of his sickness whereof he died. And Joash the king of Israel came down unto him, and wept over his face, and said, O my father, my father, the chariot of Israel, and the horsemen thereof.

Notice that Joash wasn't weeping over the fact that Elisha was sick. Joash was weeping because he and his men were about to be overtaken by Syria.

Joash was a young man when he assumed the throne. We read that he went to the aging prophet and cried for help. Imagine how desperate Joash must have been to do such a thing. In those days, kings didn't go seeking audiences with people; they gave orders and the people they wanted to see were brought to them. But Joash humbled himself and went seeking the old prophet.

Asking for Help

We learn from this passage of Scripture that the first step to overcoming disappointment, discouragement, and depression is to admit your need unashamedly.

I'm going to add a little side note here. There are some people today who need to humble themselves and seek God. Many times people in "word of faith" and charismatic circles get full of pride saying, "Well, I believed God for this, and I believed God for that. I've accomplished this, and I've accomplished that." Those people have said those kinds of things so much that now they've gotten a big head. In other words, they're thinking more highly of themselves than they ought.

Joash wasn't ashamed to weep openly in his desperation. Many times, the greatest barrier keeping us from receiving help is the pride in us that keeps us from asking for help.

So many times, Christians who find themselves in negative circumstances try to hide their situation and don't tell anyone about their problems instead of turning to their church family—the people who would be willing to reach out and minister to and help them. Sometimes Christians who are sick go to the hospital and don't let anyone know about it. If I were in that situation, there is no one else I would rather know about it than the Church. The Church can at least pray for me while I'm in there!

You see, it is your church family who will surround you with prayer and uphold you. Unfortunately, the devil gets on your shoulder, so to speak, and begins to tell you, "You better not let anyone know about this situation, or they'll think you're weak in faith."

I'm going to tell you something that may sound shocking: Everyone has been weak in faith at one time or another. It doesn't matter who you are or what your name is, how often you preach or how many people you preach to, everyone has a problem being weak in faith at some time or another. No one is on top of *everything—all* of the time.

Pride

Pride can keep us from admitting that we need someone to minister to us! It's hard sometimes to even admit to ourselves, let alone to others, that we've got a problem. Usually, other people can see for themselves that there is a problem before you ever admit it to anyone.

Have you ever gone up to a friend who you can tell is going through something and asked, "Are you doing all right? Is everything okay?" and have them tell you, "There's nothing wrong; I'm fine."? Have you ever been going through something yet answered that way when someone asked you the same thing? God may want to use that person to help us, but we're so full of pride, we won't even admit to them that we have a need.

If you aren't telling anyone that you have a problem, then there are only two ways a person can find it out. Either the Lord tells them, or you're acting so much differently than you normally do that they realize something is bothering you. Just remember, they're not asking what's wrong in order to put you down. They're asking so that they can be a help to you and minister to you.

As brothers and sisters in the Lord, we are supposed to minister to one another. Unfortunately, many Christians have come to the false conclusion that they can cope with all of their problems in and of themselves and that they don't need anyone else. But we need to realize that we can't handle everything that comes down the road by ourselves.

Trying to Hide

Sometimes you need someone to pray with you, and sometimes it just helps to talk to someone. As you talk with someone about your situation, that is often when you are able to see the way out. When I say "talk with someone," I don't mean you're crying on his or her shoulder and being negative. I mean you are just talking out the situation with someone who has a listening ear.

Too often, people are ashamed to admit that they have a problem. The problem could be anything—alcohol, drugs, lust, temper, and so forth. Unfortunately, some people have heard so much about making the proper confession, that they mistakenly have gone from the ditch of always talking negative into the ditch of trying to hide any defeats or setbacks they may be experiencing.

Getting Down

I realize that some discouragement can creep in a person's life even when they've done everything right. Just the stress and the pressure of living in a world controlled by Satan can start to get you down sometimes. For instance, working at a place where you are constantly subjected to hearing vulgar talk, the Lord's name being taken in vain, and pessimistic attitudes can wear on you over time and maybe even begin to rub off on you. That is when you need to seek some help.

Some people let themselves get down so low that they get themselves in a position where it's hard for them to believe God. If we get to that place, that's when we need others to pray the prayer of agreement with us and help us out (Matt. 18:19).

When our son, Craig, had an operation to remove a brain tumor several years ago, my wife and I didn't try to hide what we were going through. It helped to have people pray for us, love on us, and give us strength. I am glad that we had people who were willing and able to pray with us and believe God with us.

Just Admit It

I'm not ashamed to admit that I have come to the position of needing other people to pray with me. The Bible teaches me that before a person can receive any help, he has to admit that he has a need. You had to admit you were a sinner and needed a Savior before you could get saved. If you're sick, you have to admit it before you can receive healing. If you need money, you have to admit that you need it before you can get it.

Some people think that to admit we're dealing with these kinds of things means our spiritual life is in bad shape. Some people say, "Well, if they were strong spiritually, they wouldn't have any problems, and they would never need anyone to help them out." That's not so. Many people have taught that, but it's not so.

If that were so, James would not have told us to pray for one another (James 5:16). When James said that he was not talking about praying for those who weren't in the Kingdom of God. He was talking about praying for our fellow Christians.

Why are you praying for them? Usually when a prayer is offered it is because something needs to be taken care of. So when we are told to pray for one another, we know we can pray for another Christian who is in need.

Some people think that we must build ourselves up until we're such strong Christians that we never admit anything bothers us. I have yet to see anyone who is that strong. I even find in the Bible that the men who walked with Jesus had problems.

Some people today want to criticize anyone who denies the faith. Let's not forget that Peter—who actually walked and ministered with Jesus—denied the faith! You see, if you miss it and deny the faith, the important test is what you do after the rooster crows. What you do after that determines your future.

The rooster crowing simply reminded Peter who he was and what he needed to do. If you ever find yourself in this position, it can serve to remind you what you need to do. Turn to those who can minister to you, work with you, pray with you, and help you get out of the situation.

Take Action

Disappointment, discouragement, and depression can paralyze your faith. Remember, faith is action. Faith is doing something. Faith gets up, reaches out, and moves. But when you are buried under the weight of disappointment, discouragement, and depression, your faith can become paralyzed. You aren't physically paralyzed, but the circumstances you're in are affecting you mentally and emotionally to the point where they are preventing you from acting on your faith.

When you begin saying, "Oh, I don't know what to do. I don't know what to do," you are paralyzed and can't do anything! To get out of any situation that you're in you have to *do* something. You have to act.

Let's look at the story of Elisha and Joash again to learn the importance of action.

Follow Instructions

Remember, Joash went to Elisha to ask for counsel because the Israelite army was about to be taken by the Syrian army.

2 KINGS 13:14–16

14 Now Elisha was fallen sick of his sickness whereof he died. And Joash the king of Israel came down unto him, and wept over his face, and said, O my father, my father, the chariot of Israel, and the horsemen thereof.

15 And Elisha said unto him, Take bow and arrows. And he took unto him bow and arrows.

16 And he said to the king of Israel, Put thine hand upon the bow. And he put his hand upon it: and Elisha put his hands upon the king's hands.

In verse 15, we read that Elisha's instructions to King Joash were to take a bow and arrows. Imagine King Joash's response: "Elisha, I come down here for you to tell me an answer to my problem, and you tell me to get a bow and arrows." But Joash obeyed and *acted* on the word of the Lord given by the prophet.

First, Elisha told Joash to take the bow and arrows. Joash obeyed and got the bow and arrows. Then Elisha told him to put them in his hand as if to shoot an arrow. Again Joash obeyed and got the bow ready to shoot.

2 KINGS 13:15–17

15 And Elisha said unto him, Take bow and arrows. And he took unto him bow and arrows.

16 And he said to the king of Israel, Put thine hand upon the bow. And he put his hand upon it: and Elisha put his hands upon the king's hands.

17 And he said, Open the window eastward. And he opened it. Then Elisha said, Shoot. And he shot. And he said, The arrow of the Lord's deliverance, and the arrow of deliverance from Syria: for thou shalt smite the Syrians in Aphek, till thou have consumed them.

What would you have done if you were in Joash's shoes? Think about this a minute. Joash, king of all Israel, goes to the aging prophet to get some answers. The prophet starts telling him to do things that don't make any sense in the natural. Joash could have thought, *What good is it going to do to get a bow and arrows and open a window?*

Elisha's answer didn't seem to be a very good one. In fact, it sounds sort of foolish when you think about it. But Joash did as he was told, took the bow and arrows, and went over and opened the window. Then the prophet laid his hands upon Joash and told him to shoot the arrow out the window.

I want you to notice that it was only after Joash obeyed the prophet's instructions that the prophet laid his hands on him. If Joash hadn't done what the prophet said to do, the prophet wouldn't have done anything more.

Many people want some preacher to lay hands on them and pray for them, yet they haven't done anything themselves. Not only do you need to act on the Word before you have someone else lay hands on you, but then after hands are laid on you, you have to continue to do what the Word says.

Joash followed the prophet's instructions before *and* after Elisha laid hands on him.

Faith Acts

Faith is doing something–taking action. It's impossible to do something or to get into action when you're lying down. If I'm lying down, really the only thing I can do is move my arms and legs around. If I'm going to do anything else, I've got to push myself up and get up in a different position.

Believing is just as much action as it is attitude. You can mentally assent or passively agree to the doctrine of faith, but mental assent and passive agreement don't put faith into action. In other words, you can say, "I believe in healing according to what the Word of God says," but not experience healing in your life. You can even say, "I believe that Jesus

Christ is the Son of God, I believe that He is the Savior of the world," and still not allow Him to be Lord of *your* life.

When you believe something according to the Word of God, you've got to *act* on what you believe in order for what you believe to become a reality in your life.

When you are faced with disappointment, discouragement, or depression, you have to put Romans 8:37 into action.

ROMANS 8:37

37 Nay, in all these things we are more than conquerors through him that loved us.

If you believe that this scripture is true *and* act upon it, it will prove itself to be true in your life. In other words, it will manifest in the natural and you will live as more than a conqueror.

Attack!

Let's review what we've learned in this chapter so far. When problems come against you, the first thing you have to do is unashamedly *admit that you have a problem*. Second, you must *put action to your faith*. And now, third, you have to *attack the problem*.

Again, let's look at the story of Joash and Elisha to learn the importance of attacking the problem.

2 KINGS 13:18–19

18 And he said, Take the arrows. And he took them. And he said unto the king of Israel, Smite upon the ground. And he smote thrice, and stayed.

19 And the man of God was wroth with him, and said, Thou shouldest have smitten five or six times; then hadst thou smitten Syria till thou hadst consumed it: whereas now thou shalt smite Syria but thrice.

When Elisha told Joash to get the bow and arrows, open the window, and shoot, he was testing Joash's faith and obedience. Joash passed that test. But in verse 18, Elisha told Joash to take the arrows and smite, or *strike*, the ground. This was a test of persistence and determination. In this test, Joash failed.

When Elisha told Joash to strike the ground with the arrows, Joash obeyed him, but he struck the ground half-heartedly. His lukewarm attitude showed that he didn't have much zeal. And because Joash failed to keep striking the ground, he and his army would only be able to defeat the Syrians three times instead of being able to completely destroy them.

When the prophet told him to strike the ground, Joash should have kept on striking it until the prophet told him to stop.

When we are facing obstacles and circumstances, we too must keep striking the ground. It's not enough to have faith and obedience, we must also be determined to persevere no matter what! The Apostle Paul said it this way: "Therefore put on the full armour of God, so that when the day of evil comes, you may be able to stand your ground, and AFTER YOU HAVE DONE EVERYTHING, TO STAND" (Eph. 6:13 *NIV*).

Attack your problem. And when disappointment, discouragement, or depression try to come upon you, start striking the ground and don't stop until you have the victory. You see, stubborn problems don't dissolve overnight. And half-hearted attempts to get them out of your life won't work. Sometimes victory demands patience, perseverance, and determination.

Have you ever complimented someone on his accomplishment or great success and had him tell you it took a lot of "blood, sweat, and tears"? That saying describes the determination, hard work, and victory over every obstacle that it takes to accomplish something.

We need to have that same "blood, sweat, and tears" determination when we're going out to do battle against the enemy. That's the kind of attitude that will bring us victory over every obstacle.

Some people strike the ground, so to speak, for a little while but then quit when they don't see immediate results. After standing on God's Word for a little while, they say,

"Well, I guess this isn't going to work."

Because they had been striking the ground, striking the ground, striking the ground, and nothing was happening as far as they could tell, they gave up when their victory might have been in the next strike. Too many people give up just before the victory comes.

We can't afford to quit! If we quit, what are we going to win? But if we don't quit, what have we got to lose?

Keep Striking!

Attack your difficulties and keep on attacking them until you wipe them out. As I said in the beginning of this chapter, all of us deal with disappointment and discouragement. It's only when you give in to it and let it take control that you're doomed.

When disappointment, discouragement, and depression come from the outside and try to take over your mind, that's when you must let the Word come from the inside and begin to "strike the ground." I'm using the image of striking the ground figuratively. Quoting the Word is the same thing as striking the problem. Say what God's Word says about your situation. Call those things that be not as though they were—until they are (Rom. 4:17)!

If you need help today, admit you need help and don't be ashamed to ask someone to pray with you. Affirm your faith and your trust in God by doing something as an act of your faith. And hammer away at the problem until it yields underneath the relentless blows of the Word of God. This is the battle plan for defeating disappointment, discouragement, depression, or anything else that comes against you. Believe the Word, act on the Word, and keep striking the ground!

Chapter 12

Possessing What Belongs to You

Progress always involves risks.
You can't steal second and keep your foot on first.

Frederick Wilcox

＊━━━━━━＊

Sometimes it may seem impossible to possess what God says belongs to you. But the Word says that with God, *all* things are possible (Matt. 19:26)! At times, there may be barriers in your life blocking your pathway to success. So I want to share some truths from God's Word that will help you discover how to possess what belongs to you.

In Joshua chapter 1, Joshua has become Israel's leader, and for the second time, the Israelites stand surveying their Promised Land. The generation of the Israelites who had rebelled against the Lord died in the wilderness just as He said they would. The younger ones are all grown up, and they are finally ready to possess their Promised Land.

JOSHUA 1:1–11 (*NIV*)

1 **After the death of Moses the servant of the Lord, the Lord said to Joshua son of Nun, Moses' assistant:**

2 **"Moses my servant is dead. Now then, you and all these people, get ready to cross the Jordan River into the land I am about to give to them—to the Israelites.**

3 I will give you every place where you set your foot, as I promised Moses.

4 Your territory will extend from the desert to Lebanon, and from the great river, the Euphrates—all the Hittite country—to the Great Sea on the west.

5 No one will be able to stand up against you all the days of your life. As I was with Moses, so I will be with you; I will never leave you nor forsake you.

6 Be strong and courageous, because you will lead these people to inherit the land I swore to their forefathers to give them.

7 Be strong and very courageous. Be careful to obey all the law my servant Moses gave you; do not turn from it to the right or to the left, that you may be successful wherever you go.

8 Do not let this Book of the Law depart from your mouth; meditate on it day and night, so that you may be careful to do everything written in it. Then you will be prosperous and successful.

9 Have I not commanded you? Be strong and courageous. Do not be terrified; do not be discouraged, for the Lord your God will be with you wherever you go."

10 So Joshua ordered the officers of the people:

11 "Go through the camp and tell the people, 'Get your supplies ready. Three days from now you will cross the Jordan here to go in and take possession of the land the Lord your God is giving you for your own.'"

During forty years of wandering in the wilderness, Joshua and Caleb never once quit believing God. I'm sure their faith was tried and tested many times over as they wandered with those unbelieving Israelites for forty years. Think about it. Joshua and Caleb had to hang around with those unbelieving Israelites for forty years! While they talked faith, their friends and fellow workers talked unbelief. When Joshua and Caleb said, "We can," everyone else said, "We can't." But Joshua and

Caleb never gave up their faith in God because they knew that they could take the land.

The first time the children of Israel went up to possess the Promised Land, they discovered that there were giants in the land and that the cities were walled. Ten out of the twelve spies looked at the barriers and said, "We can't do it." What they said came to pass, and they wandered around in the desert for forty years.

Now, in Joshua chapter 1, a new generation of Israelites stands at the River Jordan ready to possess the land. God speaks to them through Joshua and says, "Go over, and possess the land." And yet the Jordan River stood as a barrier between them and the Promised Land.

God told the Israelites in Joshua 1:2 to cross the Jordan, but how did He expect them to cross a river? There were no bridges, and they had no boats!

Notice that even though the Israelites came up against an impossibility, God didn't tell them they could quit. You see, God turns impossibilities into possibilities.

Faith Takes Possession

Impossible barriers never bother God. We may let them have quite an affect on us, but they don't ever bother God because nothing is impossible for Him. And if you're a child of God, the power of God lives inside you, so impossible barriers shouldn't bother you either!

Any time you come up against what seems like an impossible barrier, you should immediately recognize it as just another chance for God to work. It didn't make any difference to God how deep or how wide the River Jordan was. He gave Israel a plan so that they could accomplish the impossible.

You have a plan written in the Word of God whereby you too can accomplish the impossible. God's Word contains His plan and His promises, but it's up to you to follow His plan and take possession of what belongs to you. *Faith takes possession of the promises of God.*

The Lord told Joshua, "Instruct the priests carrying the Ark of the Covenant to step into the river, and as soon as they wade into the river, it will stand up in a heap." This plan didn't make sense in the natural. It doesn't make sense to think that if you start walking into a river, the water will stand up as walls on either side of you.

The Bible tells us in Joshua 3:15 that the Jordan's waters were at flood stage at this time. In the natural we know that if we wade into water too deep for us to stand, we could drown. But when waters are at flood stage, often the river's current is strong enough to pull you under and sweep you downriver.

Hang On!

You may feel overwhelmed by the circumstances of life, and it may seem as though the circumstances are a raging flood trying to sweep you and everything you have into the current and destroy you. You may feel as though you are hanging on for dear life.

That feeling comes to us all, young and old alike. It doesn't make any difference if you're a preacher or an individual sitting in the pews and volunteering in the church. At one time or another, we've all felt as though we were just hanging on. But, friend, if you will keep hanging on, you will come out victorious on the other side.

No matter what it feels like, remember that we don't walk by feelings or by sight. We walk by what we believe. So, keep hanging on and believing God. He can make the impossible possible!

Step Into the Water

In Joshua chapter 3, we read that God made the impossible possible for Joshua and the Israelites.

JOSHUA 3:7–8 (*NIV*)

7 And the Lord said to Joshua, "Today I will begin to exalt you in the eyes of all Israel, so they may know that I am with you as I was with Moses.

**8 Tell the priests who carry the ark of the covenant:
'When you reach the edge of the Jordan's waters, go
and stand in the river.'"**

The priests were told to pick up the Ark and go stand in
the river.

If the priests had merely gone and stood at the edge of
Jordan's waters, nothing would have happened. They had been
told to stand *in* the river, so nothing happened until *they stepped
into the water.* Those priests could have stood on the bank of
the river and shouted and praised God and made confessions
all day long, and the water never would have parted.

Imagine these priests as they came up to the edge of the
water. We might not blame them if they had turned around to
Joshua and said, "Wait a minute. If we step into this water
while we're carrying this heavy Ark, we could be swept away.
We might drown. What are you trying to do to us anyway?"
But the priests didn't say that. Instead, they probably began to
remember what they had been told about their forefathers'
deliverance from Egypt. They remembered that when their
forefathers had come up against what looked like an impossible
Red Sea, God made them walk through on dry land. The
priests believed God could do the same thing for them. And so
they said, "Let's march."

Faith and Obedience

More Christians should be like these priests. Many Christians
are standing on the brink of their deliverance, but instead of
doing what God has told them to do, they're just shouting and
praising God. Now don't misunderstand me. I believe we
should shout and praise God and make faith confessions. But
we can't do all these things and expect something to happen if
we're standing still, not doing what God has told us to do.

To take possession of what God says belongs to you, you're
going to have to *do* something. If the priests had just stood at
the bank of the Jordan and never taken a step, nothing would

have happened. They had to obey God. We, too, must obey the plan He's given us. To receive from God, there are two things we have to understand: *faith* and *obedience*.

You can make your faith confession all day long, but until you obey what God has told you in His Word, nothing is going to happen! I see many people confessing the Word and talking about their faith. But they're not *doing* anything.

You see, God had told the priests to do something. They didn't just believe that God could and would part the waters; they obeyed what He told *them* to do. God told them to go stand in the water, and they did what He said!

Have you seen people at the beach who walk up to the shoreline but when a wave comes in and gets near their feet, they back up in a hurry? Or have you seen the people who want to go swimming in the pool, but the water's a little cool, so they walk up to the edge and just barely dip their toes in to test the temperature?

I'm the kind of person who would rather run and jump in. If you're going to get in, you might as well get in all the way. Some people get in the water a little bit at a time until they are finally all the way in. As far as I'm concerned, it's a whole lot easier just to jump on in! The priests had to get in the water before something happened. It may time for you to get in the water too!

Corresponding Actions

When you take the first step of obedience, something begins to happen. The Holy Spirit on the inside of you will show you how to get across the river that is at flood stage in your life.

God began to operate when the priests stepped in the water.

JOSHUA 3:15–17 (*NIV*)

15 Now the Jordan is in flood all during harvest. Yet AS SOON AS the priests who carried the ark reached the Jordan and THEIR FEET TOUCHED THE WATER'S EDGE,

16 the water from upstream stopped flowing. It piled up
in a heap a great distance away, at a town called Adam
in the vicinity of Zarethan, while the water flowing
downstream to the Sea of Arabah (the Salt Sea) was
completely cut off. So the people crossed over opposite
Jericho.

17 The priests who carried the ark of the covenant of the
Lord stood firm on dry ground in the middle of the
Jordan, while all Israel passed by until the whole
nation had completed the crossing on dry ground.

Faith *and* obedience bring God on the scene. You might be
saying, "Oh, God, bless me. God, help me; give me a job; do
such and such." Although you do need to pray and believe
God, you must also get up and begin to do something.

You see, some people who are believing God for a job are
believing that He's going to just drop one on them from
Heaven. That's not how it works. It's fine to pray and confess
that God is going to give you a job. But after you have prayed,
get up and start filling out job applications!

It's important to believe God's Word, but you also have to
do something. Many people do believe the Word, but never
add any action to their faith. James said, ". . . Show me your
faith without any deeds, and I will show you my faith by what
I do" (James 2:18 *NIV*).

Take Your Own Action

You can know how to believe God and still not receive
what you're believing for. When I was a teenager, my ear
swelled up from a severe infection. My dad prayed for me as
he always did when I had physical symptoms. I believed God
that I would be healed. Every other time my dad had prayed
for me, I was healed, but this time nothing happened when he
prayed.

To make a long story short, my dad prayed and asked the
Lord why I wasn't healed this time, and the Lord told him,

"You can't carry your son any more. He believes the Word, and it's time for him to take his own action."

You see, I was fifteen years old. Every time before that when I needed something, I just called my dad and he prayed for me. Yes, I believed the Word, but my dad would do all the praying. This time was no different. When my dad and I knelt down together, I waited for him to start praying. After a few moments of silence, I asked him, "Are you going to pray?"

He said, "No, I'm not the one who needs something. *You* do!"

Then he explained to me that I had to do my own praying. I prayed, putting action to my faith, and was healed!

Maybe you are believing God for something right now. You may need to just start out with this simple obedience: Trust God and move forward, regardless of the circumstance that surrounds you.

Someone might say, "You don't know my situation."

I don't have to know your situation. I know what God's Word says, and whatever your situation might be, it's taken care of by the Word of God. There is no situation, no circumstance, and no problem that can't be remedied by the Word of God.

Of course, the Word only works when you're in faith and obedience. Many sick people make faith confessions, saying, "The Lord has healed me. By His stripes I am healed and whole." And it's scriptural to do that! You should make those faith confessions. But then you should also put action to your faith. Begin to do something you couldn't do. If you're lying in bed saying, "I believe God has healed me," then get up out of bed and start acting the way a healed person acts.

Some people are standing at the river, saying, "Oh, God, help me." You can stand on the water's edge all day and wait for God to do something, but nothing will happen. You can confess His Word all day long, but until you put some action with it, nothing will happen.

Remember James said, "Faith without works is dead." In other words, faith without corresponding actions doesn't produce anything. Real faith begins to do something. It doesn't just sit there, doesn't just stand there. Putting action to our faith is in obedience to God's Word, and when we mix faith and obedience, we possess what belongs to us!

God Will Guide You

The Lord promised He would deliver us out of all our problems, circumstances, and trials—no matter what they may be. It makes no difference to God whether your problem is physical, financial, emotional, etc. It makes no difference to God how big or small your problem is. He will deliver you!

Just standing at the edge of the river, so to speak, looking at the turmoil all around you will not help you. Standing there wishing that things were better, thinking "I wish such and such were different," standing there merely making a confession of faith will not get you through the river to possess the land on the other side.

Those priests could have stood there all day long and nothing would have happened. If you've been standing still awhile, it's time to start marching.

You might say, "But I can't see where I'm going."

That's all right. If you speak the Word, you'll be able to see the path because Psalm 119:105 says the Word is a light unto your path. As you speak the Word, it acts as a flashlight in your life. Using a flashlight, you can't see very far down the trail, especially on a real dark night or if you're in a lot of trees—the circumstances and trials of life! But as you quote the Word, it will illuminate your path enough to show a step at a time. When you see the next step to take, take it!

"But I don't know what's out there. I don't know how the ground is."

Too many Christians don't possess what belongs to them because they're standing around saying, "Well, I don't know. Maybe . . ."

There is no "maybe" about it. God said, "Move," so move! When you learn how to step out over the aching the void of nothingness with nothing underneath you but the Word of God, you will discover that He meets you every time.

Remember, faith possesses the promises of God. God has promised us life, liberty, happiness, health, healing, wholeness, and much more. You can stand on the dry riverbank if you want to. But I'm going to move out because I want to possess what belongs to me.

ISAIAH 43:2 (*NIV*)

2   When you pass through the waters, I will be with you; and when you pass through the rivers, they will not sweep over you. When you walk though the fire, you will not be burned; the flames will not set you ablaze.

If the devil has a fire burning, just walk on through with God. He will show you the way. Begin to step, and He will lead and guide you. You may think you're going to be burned, but if you'll believe God, He will lead you through the fire. He will lead you through the river, and you will come out on the other side singing the praises of your God. He will deliver you if you will believe Him and act like His Word is so.

Don't Wait for Something to Happen

You can stand on the riverbank if you want to and never possess the land God has for you. But God doesn't want you to give up and quit. He wants you to go on. If you quit, you won't gain anything. But if you keep going and keep standing on God's Word in faith, you have everything to gain.

The enemy can tug and pull, and it may seem that he's going to pull you under. But when he comes in like a flood, the Lord will raise up a standard against him!

ISAIAH 59:19

19   So shall they fear the name of the Lord from the west, and his glory from the rising of the sun. When the enemy shall come in like a flood, the Spirit of the Lord shall lift up a standard against him.

Sometimes the enemy comes into our lives like a flood. He comes in like a fire raging and destroying. But in Isaiah 43:2, God promises us that when we pass through the water, we won't be swept under, and when we walk through the fire, we will not be burned. The enemy will try to flood your life with discouragement. He'll try to take you into bondage. Just take the Word of God and step into the river, so to speak. The Bible tells us that when the Israelites stepped into the river, it walled up on either side of them. But it wasn't until they got their feet wet that something happened!

If you've been waiting for something to happen in your life, go to God's Word and find out what He says belongs to you. Believe what His Word says, and then put corresponding action to your faith by doing what He's told you to do. It's time to get your feet wet and possess what belongs to you!

Chapter 13

Stay in the 'Jericho March'

Perseverance is not a long race;
it is many short races one after the other.

Walter Elliott

+—■◆■—+

Many of us at one time or another have missed out on possessing what God says belongs to us simply because we failed to stay in the "Jericho march." The children of Israel faced a literal Jericho. For us, Jericho represents anything that the enemy puts in our way–physically or spiritually–to prevent us from receiving what God says belongs to us.

Staying in the "Jericho march" means you will continue to do whatever God has told you to do until the walls of your Jericho come tumbling down.

JOSHUA 6:1–5 (NIV)
1   Now Jericho was tightly shut up because of the
    Israelites. No one went out and no one came in.
2   Then the Lord said to Joshua, "See, I have delivered
    Jericho into your hands, along with its king and its
    fighting men.
3   March around the city once with all the armed men.
    Do this for six days.
4   Make seven priests carry trumpets of rams' horns in

**front of the ark. On the seventh day, march around the
city seven times, with the priests blowing the trumpets.**

5 **When you hear them sound a long blast on the trumpets, make all the people give a loud shout; then the
wall of the city will collapse and the people will go up,
every man straight in."**

Just because we have God's promises to possess certain
things is no sign that possessing them is going to be easy. God
never said it'd be easy. But He did said we would possess.

These days it seems as though everyone is always looking
for something easy–the quick fix. We live in the day of fast
everything. With our modern technology, you can microwave a
potato and have dinner ready in just a few minutes. And
because of the ready-made cake mixes, it doesn't even take as
long as it used to bake a cake.

I remember my grandma made cakes from scratch. She
lived to be ninety and baked in the days when ready-made
mixes were available, but she still made her cakes from scratch.
Today, however, it seems as though most people want everything fast. We open a box, dump the contents in a bowl, add
some eggs and water, mix it, and stick it in the oven. But it was-
n't that way when Grandma did it. It took some time back then.

In this modern day of "quick and easy," many Christians
want to be able to sit down, say "Thank You, Lord," and
receive all God's blessings. But sometimes you have to get up
and put legs to your faith, so to speak.

As we saw in the previous chapter, the Israelites had to
cross the Jordan River, which seemed to them to be an impossibility. And remember that nothing happened until the priests
put their feet in the water. Well, after they crossed the Jordan,
they still didn't just sit down and take it easy. They were in the
land that God said was theirs, but they were faced with another
impossible situation.

Over the course of possessing all that belongs to you, as you
make progress and overcome one obstacle, the devil will put

another impossibility in your way. You may say, "I'm getting so tired of this." Friend, I want to tell you something. From now until Jesus comes back, we're going to have opportunity after opportunity to prove that God's Word still works!

You may have to take a Jericho march, and you may have setbacks along the way. The enemy may even seem to win a battle. But, remember, just because you lose a battle doesn't mean you lose the war. We all have setbacks, but we keep on marching. The people who sit down and cry over their situations are the ones who never get any further toward receiving the benefits that God has promised them.

The Battle Plan

In Israel's Jericho march, God gave Joshua a battle plan that didn't make sense according to normal military strategy—and Joshua was a military leader. Moses had sent him into many battles, preparing him to take over the leadership of the children of Israel. But Joshua was also a man of faith, and he knew how to trust God. So Joshua accepted God's battle plan and followed it exactly.

The battle plan was to have the priests lead the people in the march. Some priests carried the Ark of the Covenant, and on the seventh day of the march, seven priests were given rams' horns and ordered to blow them as they marched around Jericho seven times. The people were instructed to give a loud shout when they heard a long blast on the trumpets (Joshua 6:4-5).

The Israelites had been trained to fight and probably had trouble with the idea of not using their spears and other weapons to conquer Jericho. But the Israelites knew that the last time the nation didn't do what God said to do, they got in trouble and wandered in the wilderness for forty years. So even though they might not have liked the battle plan, they followed it anyway.

Don't Complain

Imagine for a moment the walled city of Jericho. This city had never been conquered. The wall of protection that surrounded the city was mammoth. Some historians say it was wide enough to race two chariots side by side on top of it. It was so wide that there were houses built into the wall.

Imagine the people of Jericho who lived in the wall looking out their windows to see masses of people marching around their wall. Imagine the watchmen on the top of the wall looking down at a bunch of people marching, blowing rams' horns, and carrying around what appeared to them to be a funny-looking chest. The people of Jericho must have thought, *What's the matter with this bunch? They don't have any spears or other kind of weapons. They're just walking around the wall. What do they think they're doing?*

The people of Jericho might have even shouted things to the Israelites, but the children of Israel kept quiet and kept walking. They walked around the city the first day, and then went back to their camp. Nothing happened; they just walked around the city.

Too many times, Christians walk around their problems expecting them to disappear. When nothing happens, they sit down and say, "Oh, God why isn't something happening?" The Israelites didn't go back to their camp and cry and complain. Instead, they got up the next day and walked around the city again.

Lean Not to Your Own Understanding

I'm sure anyone who has served in the United States armed forces would agree that whenever a regiment is sent to fight a battle, every member makes sure he has all his weapons with him. Suppose on the morning of the scheduled attack, the sergeant came by and said, "The general told the lieutenant and the lieutenant told me that we're supposed to leave all our weapons here at camp, go out where the enemy is, and march around them one time. Then we will come back to camp and sit around, and tomorrow we'll go march around them again. On the seventh day we're going to march seven times. Then at my signal,

the bugler will blow a loud blast on the bugle, at which time
everyone is to yell. And then we're going to take the enemy."
Most soldiers would say, "Sarge, you're crazy." I'm sure that
some of the soldiers in the Israelite army who had been specially
trained for combat thought, *Joshua, you have lost your mind!*

But the Israelites were trusting in the Word of the Lord.
The Word of God says, "Trust in the Lord with all your heart
and lean not on your own understanding" (Prov. 3:5 *NIV*).
The Israelites couldn't lean to their own understanding in this
situation. Their own understanding would have told them,
"You're crazy to do this silly thing." But they trusted the Lord
and stayed in the Jericho march.

Get in the March!

You need to understand that if you're going to win and
overcome, you need to get into a Jericho march! Too many
Christians are just sitting around not doing anything. Faith is
not passive; faith is *active*.

God told Israel He would give them their land. But I want
you to notice something. Joshua 1:11 says, *"Pass through the
host, and command the people, saying, Prepare you victuals; for within
three days ye shall pass over this Jordan, to go in to possess the land,
which the Lord your God GIVETH YOU TO POSSESS IT."* You
see, God gave Israel the land, but they still had to possess it.

God's already given you promises in His Word, but you
must possess them. In other words, you have to take what
belongs to you! "Possess" means *to take into one's possession; the
act of having or taking into control.* God has told us what belongs
to us in His Word; now we must take possession!

A person don't possess something by sitting still. Some
people are just sitting around, with their arms folded across
their chest, saying, "Thank You, Lord. Your Word says such and
such belongs to me. I thank You." As long as they just sit there,
n-o-t-h-i-n-g is theirs. Nothing! But when they pull themselves
up out of the chair and walk out to do a Jericho march, watch

the walls come tumbling down! Watch the circumstances of life that have blocked their way begin to disappear!

Now, it may not happen overnight. It didn't happen overnight for Israel. Remember, with God payday is not every Friday, but payday always comes. The Word of God says that one day to Him is as a thousand years (2 Peter 3:8). We need to understand that God does not operate on our twenty-four-hours-a-day, three-hundred, sixty-five-days-a-year calendar. If we could see things from God's perspective, we would probably be a lot more patient.

Speak God's Word

God didn't promise that you would never encounter some spiritual "Jerichos" when He said, "Possess the land." God never said that you weren't going to have problems. There will be tests, trials, temptations, and situations where you will have to make a decision whether you're going to sit down and quit or get up and keep having a Jericho march.

All of us have faced those type of situations at one time or another. They may bring sorrow or disappointment. We sometimes lose someone or something dear to us. But are we going to sit down and quit? Or are we going to stay in the Jericho march and come out victorious on the other side?

When we come up against impossible situations, we must keep on marching, saying what the Word of God says about the situation: "Greater is He who's in me than he who's in the world" (1 John 4:4). "I can do *all* things through Christ who strengthens me" (Phil. 4:13). "By His stripes I'm healed" (1 Peter 2:24). "In all things I'm more than a conqueror in Christ Jesus" (Rom. 8:37). "No weapons formed against me will prosper" (Isa. 54:17). "All my needs are met according to His riches in glory" (Phil. 4:19). "If God is for me, who can be against me" (Rom. 8:31)? "Thanks be unto God Who always causes me to triumph in Christ Jesus" (2 Cor. 2:14).

God's Word coming out of your mouth as you're in the Jericho march will knock down any impossible obstacle in your life. But your responsibility is to stay in the Jericho march and keep quoting the Word of God over every situation. Then you shall possess what God said belongs to you!

It doesn't matter what the problem is or how bad it hurts. God can give you the victory and you can come out on the other side of it stronger than ever! Not only will you be victorious, but you will also be able to help those who go through the same thing you went through.

We All Win in the End

I went through a tough time in 1983 when my son Craig was diagnosed with a brain tumor. Unless you've been there, you don't know the feeling that hits you in the pit of the stomach when six doctors look you square in the face and say, "Your son has a tumor the size of a lemon at the base of his brain."

Craig was in the operating room for twelve hours, and when he came out of surgery, the doctors told me, "We got most of the tumor, but there's still a little bit of the edge in there." That was tough to face! But God took care of the rest of the tumor, and we came out on the other side. Thank God for the victory! Thank God for all of His blessings and His benefits!

Unfortunately, some Christians don't win their battles. And in this life, we encounter things that we don't always completely understand. But if you are down because you lost a battle, I want to tell you that the fight still isn't over. You can walk away victorious, knowing that you are going to win in the end! And along the way, you can help many people who are in the same situation you were in.

Our Mission

Every believer on this earth has the ability to receive the fullness of God's redemptive plan. You can possess what belongs to you. You have a choice. You can go on and possess, or you can stay where you are and never take another step forward toward receiving all that God has for you.

The devil wants to come into your life to kill, steal, and destroy (John 10:10). He will do everything he can to destroy you, your business, and your life! But we must stay in the Jericho march, moving forward and never stopping. We have a job to do, and that job is to proclaim the promises of God.

Remember this: On a battlefield there are casualties. Even when we're in a fight of faith, there are casualties. But don't let injuries or casualties get you down or cause you to stop marching. It's time to get up and to do what God said to do. Don't let a casualty keep you from receiving God's best. No matter what the battle looks like, we win the war! And the blood-stained banner of Jesus Christ shall fly as the wind of the Holy Spirit blows it in the breeze.

When the enemy comes in like a flood, remember that a standard has been raised against him (Isa. 59:19). Just keep on marching. There's no time to sit down. This is not the hour to have a victory party. But this is the hour for the Church to rise to its full stature, to gird itself in full battle array, and to move out and fight the enemy on his territory—taking what belongs to us and snatching souls from a burning hell. That is our mission.

Don't Be Fooled

So what if you come up against an obstacle or a problem? Think of all the men and women in the Bible who came up against obstacles and problems. The Word of God tells us that our enemy goes about as a roaring lion, seeking whom he may devour (1 Peter 5:8). But the Word also tells us that God will deliver the righteous out of all trouble (Ps. 34:19).

Satan took Jesus on a high mountain and said, "If you follow me, You can have the world and all the pleasure it has to offer" (Matt. 4:8-9). Satan is still playing the same tricks today. He offers fun and excitement, but he doesn't tell you that the fun and excitement turns to disaster. The TV shows and the movies make alcohol and drugs look exciting. But ask the people—the former lawyers, doctors, CEOs, preachers, and so forth—who have chosen that path. They saw the glamour and the bright lights; that's the side the devil wants to show people. But go behind the scenes, and you'll find out that the path ends in destruction. Only Jesus Christ can bring life—and that more abundantly (John 10:10).

Do you want the walls that have hindered you to come down? Then begin to shout the triumph of praise. Shout praises to God when it looks like everything is dark and bleak. Faith believes, and faith praises.

God Is Greater

Getting back to Joshua and the children of Israel, they marched around the Jericho wall one time each day for six days. On the seventh day, they marched around seven times. After their seventh march around, there was a loud blast on the trumpet. At that moment the Israelites began to shout, and the walls of Jericho came down.

JOSHUA 6:20

20 So the people shouted when the priests blew with the trumpets: and it came to pass, when the people heard the sound of the trumpet, and the people shouted with a great shout, that the wall fell down flat, so that the people went up into the city, every man straight before him, and they took the city.

Instead of praising and shouting, many Christians panic when an obstacle, disappointment, or hurt comes their way. They panic and have a spirit of fear. The Word of God says we've not been given a spirit of fear, but of love, power, and a sound mind (2 Tim. 1:7). A sound mind will tell you in every situation that it's not time to panic—it's time to praise.

God is greater than any test or trial and any hurt or disappointment you might go through. God is greater than any financial burden you may be going through. Notice I'm saying, "go through." Just because you're in a situation, don't sit down and wallow in it. Go through it!

When it seems as though everything is going wrong, and the bank repossesses something, just say, "Praise God. This is another chance to prove that God will give me back more than I had before." Remember when the devil took everything away from Job? (You see, it's the devil who steals.) At the end of the story, Job had twice as much as he had before (Job 42:10)! And if you'll stay in the Jericho march, you'll come out on the other side with more than you had in the first place.

Faith *Praises*

In Acts chapter 16, we read that Paul and Silas were in jail, up against their own "Jericho wall." Paul and Silas didn't panic; instead, they praised the Lord! Most people in that situation would have said, "Paul, you invited me to go on this mission-ary trip, and look where we are now. What's the matter here? You must be out of the will of God."

Most of the time when you find that you're facing tremen-dous obstacles and tremendous circumstances, it just proves that you *are* in the will of God. Who do you think the devil tries to mess with the most? Those who are in the will of God—the people Satan knows are going to tear his kingdom apart. What's the use of messing with someone who's not going to give him a problem?

So, just stay in the Jericho march. When your adversary comes in, when you are facing every kind of obstacle you can imagine, throw your hands in the air and begin to praise God, saying, "This is just another opportunity to prove that God is still God." You see, we have the choice to succumb to defeat or to raise our hands, praise God, and stay in the Jericho march.

Acts 16:25 says, *"And at MIDNIGHT Paul and Silas prayed, and sang praises unto God: and the prisoners heard them."* To me, midnight represents two things. Number one, it represents the darkest hour of your trial. But it also means something else. Midnight means it's the last part of the night and day is just around the corner.

Someone going through a midnight trial might say, "Oh, it's so dark!"

I tell them, "That just means you need to look on the horizon because the S-o-n of God is beginning to shed His light on your pathway. And all of your trials are going to melt like a snowball in the hot July Oklahoma sunshine."

Faith praises God *during* the Jericho march.

In Due Season

I want you to notice the Israelites were commanded to march awhile before they were allowed to open their mouths. Joshua 6:10 says, "But Joshua had commanded the people, "Do not give a war cry, do not raise your voices, DO NOT SAY A WORD until the day I tell you to shout. Then shout!" (*NIV*). Too many people open their mouths too soon. Make sure you know the whole plan before you start talking.

Also, make sure you know the whole plan before you start *marching*. There is an appropriate time to march and an appropriate time to shout. The Bible says that everything has a time and a season (Eccl. 3:1).

Psalm 1:3 says, *"And he shall be like a tree planted by the rivers of water, that bringeth forth his fruit IN HIS SEASON; his leaf also shall not wither; and whatsoever he doeth shall prosper."* Maybe you are trying to bring forth fruit when it isn't the season yet. Let me illustrate it this way: When it's not the season for strawberries, you don't go to the store to buy a fresh strawberry pie. But when late spring or early summer comes, whew! A strawberry pie will taste great!

You see, if you're going to reap the crop, you have to keep marching—up and down the rows—tending to the plants until the harvest season comes. Keep marching up and down the rows proclaiming God's Word. When the season comes, begin to shout the victory, and the harvest will be reaped and produced in your life.

Look for the Victory

If the Israelites could shout and praise God when all they could do is fix their eyes on the Ark of the Covenant, how much more can we shout and praise God when the Presence of God is dwelling inside of us! But instead of shouting, too many people are sitting around, saying, "Oh, God, why?" That's not what we should be saying. We should be shouting and praising God, saying, "I trust You, Lord. I believe Your Word."

Start looking for the victory, not the answer to "Why did this happen?" And keep marching. Too many people are asking "Why?" when they should be marching. The sooner you start praising God and marching to His drum beat, the sooner you're going to come out of your trial and situation.

March on, because just over the hill, the victory awaits you. Do not slow up just because there is an obstacle in the way. But march on through the heat and the cold, and God will show you the hand of victory. March on, and you shall see that what is behind you will have no affect on you. Do not look back; do not even think about the past. The past is the past—it's over and done with. Put it away forever and march on, and God will show you great and mighty things.

Chapter 14

How to Succeed in Life

If a man is called to be a street sweeper,

he should sweep streets even as Michelangelo painted

or Beethoven composed music or Shakespeare wrote poetry.

He should sweep streets so well that all the hosts of heaven and earth

will pause to say, "Here lived a great street sweeper who did his job well."

Martin Luther King Jr.

A s we strive to take our future by storm and succeed in all that God has planned for our lives, it is important that we safeguard our efforts. You see, no matter how hard a person strives for something, failure is still a possibility unless those things that cause failure are removed at the start.

I want to share three common reasons Christians fail in life and offer some wisdom that will help you stay on course for the future.

As we read the story of Creation in the Bible, we discover that mankind was not created to fail. We know this because Genesis chapter 1 tells us that mankind was created in the image of God.

GENESIS 1:26–27

26 And God said, Let us make man in our image, after our likeness: and let them have dominion over the fish of the sea, and over the fowl of the air, and over the cattle, and over all the earth, and over every creeping thing that creepeth upon the earth.

27 So God created man in his own image, in the image of God created he him; male and female created he them.

Verse 26 says man was created to have dominion on the earth. The word "dominion" means *to rule or have authority over.* So man was created to have authority, rule, and dominion not to fail.

But we see that man (a general term for all men and women) is always stubbing his toe, so to speak, having problems, and failing. So there has to be a cause for man's repeated failures. If man is not who he was created to be doing what he was created to do, then he's doing something wrong.

When you first discover that things are not going right, you should immediately look for the root cause of the problem. Before you can correct a problem, you have to find out what is causing the problem. You may be able to *temporarily* solve the problem without finding what caused it, but unless you fix the root cause, the problem will eventually come back.

A Temporary Solution

Once when the lights on one of our ministry busses weren't working due to some sort of electric problem, our mechanic rigged the wires so the lights would work so we could use the bus temporarily. But because he didn't fix the *cause* of the problem, what he did was only a "Band-Aid," not a permanent solution.

To learn the exact cause of the problem, the bus had to be brought into the shop and thoroughly examined, using all sorts of tools and instruments. We made the bus lights work for a little while without taking it apart, but until we addressed the root cause, it was only a temporary solution.

Many Christians are grabbing hold of the Word of God in faith and temporarily putting the devil out of business. But let's quit putting him out of business only temporarily, and let's take the Word of God straight to the cause, and put the devil out of business forever.

The Right Way

The first reason Christians fail is because they *sin*, or *transgress God's Word*. Not obeying God's Word will cause a Christian to fail. Obedience to God's Word brings success every time.

I think we all realize that not doing what God says to do can cause us to fail. But sometimes we don't realize that even if we are doing the right thing, if we are doing it the wrong way, we are in disobedience.

One example of this is found in First Samuel chapter 15. King Saul did the right thing by sacrificing to God. But he did it the wrong way by offering enemy spoils as his sacrifice.

God told Saul very specifically to do something, and Saul didn't do it. Saul became arrogant and willfully disobeyed God. If you will study the Old Testament, you will discover that often after a victory in battle, Israel would bring back the spoil and offer it to God. But before this particular battle, God commanded Saul and the people of Israel not to take any spoil from the enemy.

Saul disobeyed God's command and brought back spoil. He thought he'd make his actions okay by bringing the spoil to the prophet Samuel to offer in sacrifice to God. But Samuel said to Saul, "Obedience is better than sacrifice" (1 Sam. 15:22). In other words, it is better to obey God and do what he says than to offer Him a sacrifice.

You see, many times we fail, not because we're doing the wrong thing, per se, but because we're doing the right thing in the wrong way. To obey and do it the right way is really the only way to do it.

Count the Cost

The second reason Christians fail is because they *start something before gathering all the facts.* This is something that affects a lot of Christians and causes failure perhaps more than anything else does.

LUKE 14:28–30 (*NIV*)

28 "Suppose one of you wants to build a tower. Will he not first sit down and estimate the cost to see if he has enough money to complete it?

29 For if he lays the foundation and is not able to finish it, everyone who sees it will ridicule him,

30 saying, 'This fellow began to build and was not able to finish.'"

If you read on to verse 33, you will see that Jesus is teaching that if someone is going to follow Christ, then he must give everything he has and follow God. If you are going to follow God, you can't hold one part of your heart back, and say, "Okay, God, You can have ninety percent, but ten percent is mine." No, you must give it all to God.

That is one way to look at this passage of Scripture, but we could learn something else from these verses. Whenever we begin to do something for God, we must first sit down and study it closely to be sure that we have what it takes to finish the project. Otherwise, we're going to give Christianity (and the faith message especially) a black eye, so to speak. We will give Christians a bad name when we could have prevented doing so.

Many times it isn't a lack of faith that causes Christians to fall short. It's a lack of proper planning and preparation. When you do not calculate everything before you begin, problems arise.

I'm talking about counting the cost looking at the facts. We have to understand that there are facts that have to be looked at. It doesn't matter how much faith you have, you still have to consider the natural facts.

I want you to understand that I am not downplaying the role of faith and believing God. I am a person of faith, and I understand that believing God is a major part of what it takes to accomplish anything. But I also understand that we must sit down and count the cost before we involve ourselves in a particular project or move or decision.

As you have opportunities to do this, that, or the other, you will notice that God doesn't always tell you what to do. You may pray to get direction, but sometimes God will allow you to make your own decision when it doesn't affect your salvation or what He wants you to do. But before you make your decision, be sure you check all the details and count the cost.

Many Christians make rash decisions and then suffer the consequences. If you are thinking about quitting what you're doing to go on to something else, examine all the facts before you make your move.

Check the Facts

One man told me, "I'm going to quit my job and start my own such and such business."

I said to him, "Well, have you thoroughly checked out everything?"

(Now don't misunderstand me. This man wasn't wanting to sin or do something wrong. No matter what he decided, he was still saved. And he was still attending and volunteering in church.)

He told me, "Yes, I've checked it out pretty good. I'm believing that God will take care of everything."

I said, "God doesn't work that way."

He said, "What are you talking about?"

I explained to him that God is not going to go around sweeping up behind him and taking care of him just because he didn't use the brain God gave him to use. God created each of us with a brain, and He wants us to use it!

I thank God for faith, and I live by faith and preach faith as strongly as anyone. But we should also look at the facts and use the brain God gave us.

Now if you look at the facts and the facts say "Don't do it," and then God tells you to go ahead and do it anyway, then arm yourself with the *greater* facts of God's Word and go ahead. But you better be sure that it was God who told you to do it.

This individual who was going to quit his job to start his own business hadn't examined all the facts. When I asked him if he had done such and such and checked such and such, he said he had. But I could tell he hadn't checked anything. So I said, "If you quit your present job, how are you going to pay to start this new business?"

He said, "I've saved up some money to use for that."

I said, "Great. So you have the money to pay for the building and inventory. But what are you going to buy groceries with? How are you going to pay your house payment and your insurance? What you going to give your kids for their school expenses?"

He said, "I figure that we'll make such and such an amount the first day and by the end of the first month, we'll be clearing such and such an amount."

I asked, "Where are you getting all these estimates?"

"Well, that is what a similar store did in such and such town," He replied.

I told him, "You can't guarantee that your store will do the same."

Then he said, "You're just putting a damper on my faith."

I said, "Brother, faith doesn't have anything to do with this. I'm talking about the cold hard facts of reality."

Unfortunately, many Christians jump out and do things without proper planning and preparation. And then when they fail, they turn around and say, "God let me down. God failed me."

God didn't fail them. They failed because they didn't do what the Word of God told them to do to begin with, and that is to count the cost. Before we start something, we should do what Luke 14:28 says: Sit down first and see if we have what we need to finish what we start.

God Never Fails

Man may fail, but God never fails. And man usually fails because he didn't do what God told him to do in the first place. Maybe he didn't sit down and make sure ahead of time that he had everything in line and that he could complete the project.

Now even if you have examined the facts and know that you are able to complete the project, unforeseen things will still come up that you will overcome by exercising your faith in God.

We live in two worlds, and we have to be able to work in two worlds simultaneously. The principles of success that you use in the spirit world are the same principles you need to use in the natural world. You wouldn't dream of doing anything without being armed with God's Word, because every time the devil sticks his head up, you can put him down with the Word. Likewise, you shouldn't dream of doing a natural project without being armed with both God's Word and natural facts. That way every time there is opposition, you have the facts and the Word to fight with.

Don't misunderstand me. I'm not taking anything away from the power of God. I'm just showing you another area where one of my favorite sayings applies: "The natural and the supernatural coming together make an explosive force for God." It's not one or the other; it's both of them working together that make the explosive force for God.

Running Off 'Half-Cocked'

Jumping into something before you are ready is sometimes referred to as "running off half-cocked." That expression comes from the fact that a gun doesn't shoot like it should unless it's fully cocked. Half-cocked won't do you a bit of good. As a matter of fact, it could do you some harm.

When an F-16 fighter leaves the base for its mission, it is the duty of the ground personnel to make sure that it is armed with every available weapon it can carry. If it's supposed to carry four rockets and they only arm it with two, that pilot could be in serious trouble.

Suppose the pilot gets in a dogfight against three enemy planes. He fires the two rockets and downs two of the enemy planes. He then closes in on the third plane, has it in his sights, and pushes the button to release another rocket.

When nothing happens, the pilot says to himself, *I know I only used two rockets. I'm supposed to have two more.* The pilot then realizes that he's out of firepower with one enemy plane still flying. He starts hoping he's fast enough to outfly the enemy plane.

Now if that pilot gets shot down, people might say he failed on his mission. But the trouble didn't start when the enemy showed up. The trouble started while the plane was still on the ground, and someone didn't take care of business by fully arming the plane.

When you are thinking about getting involved in doing a project for God, remember this story about the fighter planes. God may have told you to do something, but if you don't wait around long enough to get fully armed, and instead run off ill-prepared, you will probably fail. And the failure will not be God's fault. God called; God said do it, but you didn't stay put long enough to get fully armed.

Don't Run Out of Gas

Not only does a fighter pilot need a full set of weapons, but he needs a full tank of gas in case he has to outfly the enemy.

I'm an avid racecar fan, and I love watching NASCAR races on television. In every race, the drivers have to make pit stops to refuel because their tanks don't hold enough fuel to get them through the entire race.

I remember one race in particular. The driver who had been leading the race had just left his pit stop, and the people in the pits were all frantic because they knew that he had left the pit before they finished putting enough fuel in his tank. There were not enough laps remaining for him to have time to take another pit stop, get more fuel, and still win the race. His only hope was to stay on the track and hope he didn't run out of gas.

With one lap to go, the driver came around the first corner and started down the backstretch. On the backstretch, his car began to slow down. One car passed him; then another; then another. He coasted across the finish line and finished in fourth place. Because he didn't stay in the pits the extra two seconds to get the amount of fuel that he needed, he lost the race.

Don't get in such a hurry to go out and do something that you make your move before your spiritual "tank" is full. You need to be sure you have enough of God's Word in you to keep you strong all the way to the finish line. Otherwise, you will look real good for a while but end up losing. When that happens the devil gets glory, not God.

Never Give Up!

So far we've learned that one reason many Christians fail is because they transgress God's Word or because they do the right thing the wrong way. Another reason Christians fail is because they do not observe the natural facts they jump into something without proper preparation. And a third reason many Christians fail is they *give up too soon and quit.*

The Word says that after having done all, we're to stand (Eph. 6:13). Sometimes when Christians pray but don't see immediate results, they say, "I've been praying and believing God. I guess nothing's going to happen." And they quit! Then they want to blame God and say God failed. No, God didn't fail. They gave up and quit!

We wouldn't have most of the things we have today if the men and women who invented them had given up along the way. Take the light bulb, for instance. Thomas Edison tried and tried experimented and tested to develop a practical incandescent light bulb. Today every home in the country has this kind of light bulb. But if Edison had given up after he failed the first ten, fifty, a hundred times he would never have found success.

But he kept believing. He said, "I believe that we can have a light bulb and do away with these lanterns." And he kept on trying. Today, the light bulb is internationally recognized as a symbol of creative ideas.

You probably know Babe Ruth as the "homerun king." But Babe Ruth was also the strikeout king. Ruth holds the record for more career strikeouts than any other one player. But just because he struck out doesn't mean he quit swinging. He kept swinging and swinging and swinging, and he became a baseball legend for the number of homeruns he hit.

In one game, Ruth went to the plate three times and struck out all three times. When he went to the plate for the fourth time, he swung just as hard as he did the other three times. But this time there were men on base. Ruth put the ball over the fence, helping his team win the game. Everyone forgot about the three times he struck out; they only remembered the game-winning homerun.

Problems Will Come

When you overcome obstacles and get the victory, people forget all about the past. They only remember the success. But you must understand that you're going to have some obstacles before you have the success.

Sometimes people think that if they're saved and living by faith, they will never have any problems. I wonder if those people have ever read the Book of James. The Bible says, "Consider it pure joy, my brothers, whenever you face trials of many kinds, because you know that the testing of your faith develops perseverance" (James 1:2–3 *NIV*).

Perseverance and patience come by doing the same thing over and over and over again. Problems will come, but your faith will see you through to victory if you won't quit. Remember, you cannot be defeated if you will not quit!

How to Handle Failure

The effects of failure can be devastating. It can affect your mind to the point where you can't think straight. It can affect your emotions, making you dull, gloomy, and despondent. Failure can also sap your strength and stamina and cause you to feel insecure. All of these things become the devil's playground as he tries to wreak havoc in your life.

When you stay with God in His "playground," you have strength and stamina. When you stay with God and His Word, no matter what comes or goes, you can do all things through Christ who strengthens you (Phil. 4:13).

We've discussed three causes of failure in order to help you safeguard yourself against failure. But what happens if you *do* miss it? Do you know how to handle failure?

The first thing to do when you discover that you have made a mistake is to seek divine guidance. If you don't know exactly where you missed it, then ask the Holy Spirit to show you. The Bible says that He searches our innermost parts (Prov. 20:27). The Holy Spirit will show you where you made your mistake.

If you already know where you made the mistake or the Holy Spirit has already shown you, then before you can have any success in the future, you must go back to where you made the wrong turn and start again from there.

All Turned Around

Many years ago, my wife and I got lost while driving from Texas to Springfield, Missouri. Someone had told me about a shortcut through Tulsa that would take me to Interstate 44 while avoiding the morning rush-hour traffic.

Well, I got lost. And stubborn me, I wouldn't go back to where I made the wrong turn. I wanted to keep driving and figure it all out myself. After two and a half hours of wandering

161

around, I finally found myself on Interstate 44. How I did it, I don't know. I couldn't do it again even if I wanted to.

But all I had to do was go back to where I made the wrong turn and then follow the signs and I would have been only half an hour away from Springfield. But, no, I wanted to take someone's word about a shortcut and go my own way. So after driving two and a half hours, I was still three hours from Springfield.

Sometimes we as Christians do this very thing. Instead of admitting that we missed it and saying, "Lord, I'm going to retrace my steps and go back to where I made the mistake. And then I'm going to start again from there," we wander around somewhere, saying, "Well, I believe that if I go this way and then this way, I can eventually get back to where God wanted me." So we wander around for a while, and most of the time we do end up pretty close to where we were. But all that time we spent wandering around was wasted time.

Think how much more you can accomplish if you will just admit that you messed up and then immediately turn around and get back on track.

Making Lemonade

The Apostle Paul said, "I know what it is to be in need, and I know what it is to have plenty. I have learned the secret of being content in any and every situation, whether well fed or hungry, whether living in plenty or in want" (Phil. 4:12 *NIV*). What was Paul's secret? He knew how to be content in all circumstances.

I like to say it this way: "When life gives you lemons, make lemonade." In other words, when problems come, don't become sour on life, on God, and on everything else. Instead, take what life gives you, add the Word of God, and make it something sweet!

Keep on Keeping On

Many times we look at something and think we've failed when we really haven't. Joseph is a good example of this.

Joseph did his best and got thrown in jail. He lived right, stayed true to God, and ended up in prison.

Someone might say, "Poor Joseph. What a sad story." No, it wasn't a sad story at all. It looked like a failure, but Joseph kept believing God and eventually became the prime minister of Egypt.

If Joseph had quit on God, he would never have been prime minister of Egypt. Even though it looked as though serving God had gotten him in trouble, Joseph never gave up.

Sometimes, it may look as though serving God has gotten you in trouble. But keep on serving and believing God, and God will see you through the situation. As the old saying goes, "Winners never quit, and quitters never win."

When you're in church and the pastor quotes Philippians 4:13, it's easy to believe that you can do all things through Christ who strengthens you. But do you believe it when you don't have the preacher to pump you up when you're out there by yourself and the devil has kicked you on both shins, slapped both sides of your face, and knocked you in the head? Can you still look up and say, *"I can do all things through Christ which strengtheneth me"*? Whether or not you believe it and can say it at that moment will determine if you will win.

We are nothing in ourselves, but we are everything in God. We were never intended to fail, but we will fail if we don't know how to successfully deal with whatever the devil may throw in our path.

No matter how bad you think you've failed, God wants to deliver you from the past and propel you toward the future. It's time for you to let God pick up the pieces and help you start all over again this time headed for success!

Chapter 15

What to Do When You Don't Know What to Do

All heaven is waiting to help those who discover the will of God and do it.

J. Robert Ashcroft

━┅━❈━┅━

In the "Peanuts" comic strip, Peppermint Patty once asked Charlie Brown if he knew any good rules for living. This was his list: "Keep the ball low. Don't leave your crayons in the sun. Use dental floss every day. Don't let the ants get in the sugar. And always get your first serve in."

Many people today are asking the question "What should I do?". One reason it's now very popular to ask for advice is because when people act upon advice they've been given and something bad happens, they can just blame the person who gave them the advice. Some people who ask "What should I do?" simply want someone to give them a list of things to do. Then they will have someone to blame if everything goes wrong, thereby relieving themselves of personal responsibility.

Because people have always come to the Church to ask what they should do, many churches have developed a formal list of "dos and don'ts." You may have been in a church like that. Most of the stuff on the list you wouldn't do anyway if you just read the Bible. But for some reason, people prefer to have a list of rules to follow.

It's been said that God gave Moses 613 rules to follow. In fact, if you will study the Old Testament, you will find that there are more than the Ten Commandments we are accustomed to hearing. The Mosaic Law contained many dos and don'ts.

One Law

When Jesus came, He gave us a New Covenant and a new law. No longer do we follow a long list of dos and don'ts. In this New Testament law, there are only two commands. This new law is the law of love.

Jesus gave us this law in Mark chapter 12. One of the teachers of the Mosaic Law came to ask Jesus a question. Being so familiar with the Law, this man was probably a Pharisee. He wanted Jesus to tell him which commandment was the most important.

MARK 12:28–34 (*NIV*)

28 **One of the teachers of the law came and heard them debating. Noticing that Jesus had given them a good answer, he asked him, "Of all the commandments, which is the most important?"**

29 **"The most important one," answered Jesus, "is this: 'Hear, O Israel, the Lord our God, the Lord is one.**

30 **Love the Lord your God with all your heart and with all your soul and with all your mind and with all your strength.'**

31 **The second is this: 'Love your neighbour as yourself.' There is no commandment greater than these."**

32 **"Well said, teacher," the man replied. "You are right in saying that God is one and there is no other but him.**

33 **To love him with all your heart, with all your understanding and with all your strength, and to love your neighbour as yourself is more important than all burnt offerings and sacrifices."**

34 **When Jesus saw that he had answered wisely, he said to him, "You are not far from the kingdom of God." And from then on no one dared ask him any more questions.**

If you ever wonder what you should do with your future, I will make it simple: Do what the Bible says. "Love the Lord your God with all your heart, with all your soul, with all your mind, and with all your strength. And love your neighbor as yourself" (Mark 12:30–31).

In any given situation, when you have to decide whether or not to do something and you wonder if what you might do is right or wrong, just examine the situation in light of the law of love. Ask yourself this question: "If I decide to go through with such and such, will that be loving the Lord with all my heart and soul and strength and loving my neighbor as myself?" If you ask yourself that question every time, you don't even have to ask whether the situation is right or wrong. The law of love will never lead you to sin.

The Law of Love

So many times Spirit-filled, Bible-believing, tongue-talking, "faith" people want to ask a pastor, or someone they consider an elder in the Lord, if what they want to do is right or wrong. If you're living in line with the law of love, you don't need to ask that question. But as a little side note, if you're living right with God, following His Word, doing what He says to do, being who He says to be, and so forth, and you still have to ask if something is right, then it's probably not.

You see, these two commandments—love the Lord your God and love your neighbor as yourself—are a complete conduct guide for Christians to live by. Most people want to make it complex, but the Word of God is a very simple Book to understand if you will read it with an open heart and not with glasses tinted by man's religious tradition.

Sometimes people ask, "What should I do?" because their minds are cluttered with what other people have said. But the Bible makes it simple: Love God and love your fellow man. That's it!

When you love someone, you don't steal from them, gossip about them, or lie to them. This is how the law of love guides our conduct. And yet there is no legalism in the law of love. There is no list of dos and don'ts, saying, "You have to do this," or "Don't do that."

Love Can't Be Forced

Love can't be legislated. Love isn't something you can be forced to do. It's something you begin to do by saying, "I will obey God." Love is strictly a situation of obedience to what God said to do.

I can't force you to love God and to love your neighbor. No one can! If I were stronger than you, I could probably force you to *say* that you loved God and your neighbor, or fellow man. And if I were stronger than you, or had leverage for some reason, I might make you say good things about someone. But you will only say these things as long as I am present and applying pressure. The minute you're away from me, you will say what you want to say and do what you want to do.

When my kids were growing up, I wasn't as concerned about how good my kids acted while I was around as I was about how they acted when I wasn't nearby. Sure, they would behave as long as Daddy was there. But the mark of whether or not I did a good job raising them was how they acted when they were away from me.

In the same way, love is something that has to be a part of you. When it's your way of life, you love no matter who is around.

Jesus said love is to be our rule of conduct. If you love God and love your neighbor, you will find that everything will fall into place.

A Change of Heart

The secret to an abundant life is a change of heart, not a change of mind. Many people change their mind about what they believe, but abundant life comes from having a change of heart. You see, I can change my *mind* about whether Dr. Pepper, IBC Root Beer, Pepsi-Cola, Coca-Cola, or Sprite is my favorite drink, but what's that got to do with anything? What I change in my heart is what's most important.

We must understand that everything we do is controlled from the inside out, not from the outside in. And this is where Christians need to get hold of some things. Love is the result of an inward transformation. That *inward transformation* causes an *outward reformation*. It's just as the song says: "Something on the inside working on the outside. Oh, what a change in my life."

Trying to change the inside by changing the outside will never work! The inside has to reform the outside if there is to be any lasting change.

Suppose you went to a ranch where the owners stabled a retired racehorse. In his prime, the horse won two or three races, but then developed a knee problem. He's still a good horse; he just can't race. And suppose there were also some donkeys stabled at the ranch.

Now you could take those donkeys, polish their hooves, give them a bath to clean them up, and put oil on their coat and make them look really good. And you could leave the racehorse out in the pasture to roll around and get dirty, then line both the donkey and the racehorse at a starting gate. When the bell sounds and the gates open, that racehorse will be gone—galloping down the track. The donkey, on the other hand, may run and he may not.

Why will it happen this way? I mean, the donkey looks great on the outside—much better than the horse looks. Yes, but what makes the racehorse a racehorse is not the way he looks, but what's on the inside of him.

Many people can look good on the outside. The New Testament Pharisees were a group of men who had "looking good" down pat. To paraphrase in modern language what Jesus told the Pharisees, "You look good. You look like a Christian. You smell like a Christian. But on the inside you're still a sinner" (Matt. 23:27). Remember, it's what's in the heart that counts.

Love in Action

These two principles—loving God and loving your neighbor—are not only matters of the heart, but of behavior. Love begins in the heart, but when what's on the inside changes the outside, love becomes an action. The way you act toward someone reveals the way you feel about him or her in your heart.

If you love God, then you obey His Word (John 14:15). If you love God, you won't forsake the assembling of yourself together with other Christians (Heb. 10:25). If you love God, you will pay your tithes and give offerings (Mal. 3:10). Many people say they love God, but their actions do not demonstrate love.

The only time some people show love is when they have a need. Sometimes children use this kind of manipulation with their parents. A guy I used to know treated his parents this way.

This boy's parents were well off financially, and he never gave them the time of day, so to speak, until he needed a new car or something else. When he wanted something from them, he began to visit them and tell them how much he cared for them and loved him. He did this only until he got what he needed, and then his parents didn't see him again until the next time he needed something.

This is the way many of God's children are acting toward Him. They live their own life and do their own thing, until they get in a bind or in some kind of trouble. Then they're in church every time the doors open, praying and seeking God.

Once God delivers them out of the situation, they start missing a Sunday here and a Wednesday night there, until, the next thing you know, they're not going to church at all. But if you asked them if they love God, they would say, "Oh, yes, I still love God." They don't love God—their behavior says otherwise.

The Golden Rule

When we love someone we do what we can to help him. Jesus gave us a great way to remember how to treat people. People often call it the Golden Rule, but it's found in Luke 6:31, which says, "Do to others as you would have them do to you" (*NIV*).

What are we to do? We are to love God with all of our heart—everything about us. And we are to love our fellow man, doing unto others as we would have them do unto us.

Before you ever say a word or react to an individual who is facing any circumstance of life, ask yourself this question, "If I were in his situation, how would *I* want to be treated?" If you answer this question honestly, it will probably change the way you treat that person.

Make a decision right now that if you hear people talking about someone else, saying how he messed up or did such-and-such, you will ask yourself, "How would I want people to treat me and talk about me if I were in the same situation?" You will probably decide to pray for that person in trouble instead of joining the conversation and listening to gossip.

People who gossip often say, "If it were me in that situation, I know I would never have done anything like So-and-so did!" You don't know what you would have done because you've never been in that person's shoes. So instead of passing judgment, follow the Golden Rule and treat others the way you would want them to treat you.

The Code of Love

I remember a story that poignantly illustrates the value of doing unto others as you would have them do unto you.

Many years ago, two young men were working their way through college and needed money. They came up with the idea to have Paderewski, the renowned Polish pianist and composer, give a piano recital on their college campus. They contacted his agents and learned that he wanted a guarantee of two thousand dollars.

The boys agreed to his terms and decided to go ahead with the recital. They put all their efforts into planning the event, but they only sold sixteen hundred dollars worth of tickets.

They contacted Paderewski and told him, "We only raised $1600 total, and we'll give you all of that. We'll also give you a promissory note saying that we'll pay you the other $400 as soon as we can."

Paderewski replied, "No, boys. That won't do at all." Then he tore up the promissory note, returned the money, and said, "You boys take out your expenses, give yourself ten percent of the balance, and let me have the rest."

Paderewski went ahead with the concert.

The years rolled by. World War I came and went. And Paderewski became a noted statesman in Poland. He was striving to feed the starving people of his war-ravaged country, and he asked the United States for help. As a result, thousands of tons of food from the U.S. poured into Poland. Paderewski journeyed to Paris to thank U.S. President Herbert Hoover for the relief Hoover had sent to him.

"That's all right, Mr. Paderewski," Hoover replied. "I knew the need was great. Besides, you helped me once when I was a college student."

You don't always see a quick return on the love and kindness you show. But if you sow love, you will reap love (Gal. 6:7).

As Christians we are to live by the code of love. We are to love God with everything we are and with everything we have. And we are to love people in thought, in word, and in deed.

The answer to the question "What should I do?" isn't complex, dramatic, or comprised of forty-five dollar words. It's very simple: Love God with all of your heart. Love your neighbor and do unto others as you would have them do unto you. When you follow the law of love, you will live the abundant life and find a joy and peace that you never had before.

Chapter 16

What Is Your Destiny?

Destiny is no matter of chance. It is a matter of choice:
It is not a thing to be waited for; it is a thing to be achieved.

William Jennings Bryan

D id you know you have a destiny? Do you know what your destiny is?

While it's true that every man, woman, and child has a destiny, not everyone is aware of that fact. And then there are some people who know that they have a destiny, but don't know what their destiny is.

Jesus knew *exactly* what His destiny was. And everything He did throughout His life was to fulfill that specific destiny.

JOHN 18:37

37 Pilate therefore said unto him, Art thou a king then? Jesus answered, Thou sayest that I am a king. To this end was I born, and for this cause came I into the world, that I should bear witness unto the truth. Every one that is of the truth heareth my voice.

Pilate asked Jesus, "Are you a king?" And Jesus answered, "To this end I was born." We could say it another way: "Toward this cause I was born" or "for this purpose I was born." In other words, Jesus was saying, "This is why I came to earth."

Jesus certainly understood His destiny. He knew His destiny because the Word of God says that He was slain before the foundation of the world. Jesus knew why He came to earth, and He knew all along what He was going to do.

Jesus was born to be our Savior and to save the world from their sin. What were *you* born to be and do? Whether we know it or not, God has a purpose for each of us and something for everyone to do.

God has a specific destiny for all of us. He has destined for some people to be successful business people, to make money so they can help send missionaries and support churches.

God has a destiny for everyone in every walk of life. God wants people in every walk of life to represent Him. Unfortunately, many people are in a position where they're supposed to be representing God, but they're not. They're representing the wrong kingdom.

Good Works

God cares so much about you that He has prepared a special plan for your life. Ephesians 2:10 tells you what you were created to do.

EPHESIANS 2:10 (*NIV*)
10 For we are God's workmanship, CREATED IN CHRIST JESUS TO DO GOOD WORKS, which God prepared in advance for us to do.

According to this verse of Scripture, God had things already prepared in advance for each one of us. Many people never find out what it is that God has prepared for them, so they never get on the right path of doing what God wants them to do.

Many people end up doing things that they want to do. This even happens in ministry. Someone might say, "I want to be a pastor." Well, God may not be calling him to be a pastor. Maybe he's supposed to be an associate pastor. And there's nothing wrong with being a good associate pastor. Behind every good senior pastor, there is a good associate pastor.

Know Where God Wants You

Some of us need to find out where God wants us. Not everyone is supposed to be in a leadership position. Wouldn't we be in a mess if everyone was a leader? Who would do the work?

We need to know our purpose. We must get involved with our destiny. It's time to make up our minds that we are going to fulfill our God-given destiny and no one else is going to talk or move us out of it.

Many people get in the mess they're in because when someone comes up and says, "You know you ought to be doing this," they listen and obey!

People come up to me all the time and say, "RHEMA ought to be doing this and that."

I reply, "If you want it done, maybe you should do it. That's not what God told us to do. And God is our leader."

There are too many people who are wearing a mask instead of getting real with God. They aren't real with themselves or with the people around them. They're always trying to be something they're not. God has a destiny for you. Find out what that destiny is and fulfill it, but be what God wants you to be—not what someone else wants you to be.

Fivefold Ministry Isn't for Everyone

I've been in and around ministry all of my life. And I want to tell you something. As a child, I never planned to be a preacher when I grew up. I didn't intend to be in the ministry. My son Craig always wanted to be a businessman until the night God called him to preach through a supernatural experience. Craig came home from a youth meeting one night and couldn't talk in English for two hours. When he could finally speak, he said, "God changed my plans."

God has a plan for everyone's life, but God doesn't have fivefold ministry planned for everyone. Where would the church be without the people of the congregation who are faithful to volunteer in the church and faithful in their giving?

175

Without tithes and offerings, where would ministries be? Where would the Kingdom of God be? Thank God for each individual call.

I came into this world September 3, 1939, and I lived my life in a preacher's home. I saw too much as a kid. I heard the way people talked about my dad and other preachers. I decided I did not want to be a preacher.

But one day when I was seventeen and at a youth camp, God got hold of my heart. That day, I began to realize that His destiny for my life didn't coincide with my destiny for my life.

Maybe God has a destiny for you that doesn't coincide with the destiny that you have planned for yourself. Are you willing to set aside your own destiny in order to fulfill the destiny God has for you?

Jesus knew why He came to earth. And the Word of God tells us one reason why we are on this earth. Ephesians 2:10 says, "For we are God's workmanship, created in Christ Jesus to do good works, which God prepared in advance for us to do" (*NIV*). The reason we were created in Christ Jesus was to do good works—good works that God prepared in advance for us to do!

Learn to Listen

Some people have the problem of never listening to God long enough to receive anything from Him. Some people come in the prayer line to be prayed for, and they don't receive anything because they never stop talking in order to receive. It's all right to say, "Lord, I receive." But some people are in the prayer line saying, "Lord, You know what I need. Lord, You can help me. Lord, Lord, You know what I need." They're putting out so much trying to get what they need that they never receive it.

It's great to pray, and we need to pray, but some people need to learn to be quiet and to listen to what God is saying. A conversation is not a monologue. A conversation is two people talking to one another. And if you want to have a conversation with God, you should talk a little while and then be quiet and listen to what He has to say! That is usually the way you discover your destiny and God's plan for your life.

No one is going to prophesy you into your destiny. God will speak to your own heart. If someone does prophesy something over your life that doesn't coincide with what is already in your heart, then put that "prophecy" on the shelf and forget it!

Created to Help

At the New Birth, you were created in Christ Jesus to do good works. Let's look at Ephesians 2:10 again.

EPHESIANS 2:10 (*NIV*)
10 For we are God's workmanship, created in Christ Jesus to do good works, which God prepared in advance for us to do.

Notice the verse doesn't say, "And we are God's workmanship, created in Christ Jesus to go through life twiddling our thumbs and singing, 'Hallelujah, I'm on my way to Heaven.'" No! We were created to do good works! One of the good works is reaching the world with the Gospel of the Lord Jesus Christ, telling the world that Jesus saves, Jesus heals, and Jesus is coming again.

We were created to tell people that Jesus is the answer to their problems and to minister to those in need. We were created to help our brothers and sisters. Unfortunately, there are too many people who want to just give a scripture to those who are down and say, "God bless you; have faith." The Bible says that if you have the means to help that individual and don't do it, you're worse than an infidel.

It's real easy to give someone a scripture, but it's another thing to reach in your money clip and give him a twenty, fifty, or hundred-dollar bill. Some of the greatest joys I have had have come when I am preaching somewhere and the Lord speaks to me about blessing someone with money. Sometimes after I have prayed for people in the prayer line and everyone is still praising the Lord, the Lord will point one of them out to me and say, "That individual needs some money." Unbeknownst to the person, I walk over, reach in my pocket, and while he is praising the Lord, I slip some money into his coat pocket. Later he'll probably put his hand in his coat pocket, find the money, and shout, "Praise the Lord!"

Now God isn't going to create money in a person's pocket. But if He needs to, He will lay it on someone else's heart to put some money in that person's pocket.

One time as I slipped money into someone's pocket, another minister saw me do it. Three or four weeks later, the minister told me, "I knew where that person was in life. You didn't know anything about him; you just flew into town to preach. But if he hadn't received what you put in his pocket that night, he would have lost his car."

God has called each of us to do something. We must learn to respect everyone's destiny. For example, a pastor's destiny is to care for the members of the congregation and to make decisions regarding the administration of the church. But isn't it funny how everyone thinks he knows how the church is supposed to be run. That's not their destiny. Their destiny is to be like Aaron and Hur and to hold up the pastor's hands—to help and support him, not to tell him what to do!

Divine Purpose

What is your destiny? Whether or not you know it, you have a divine purpose. God created you to do more than breathe oxygen and take up space—He has a plan for your life!

The Psalmist David said, "I will praise You for I'm fearfully and wonderfully made . . ." (Ps. 139:14). Some people are always complaining that they're too short or too tall, too big in the waist or not big enough. When was the last time you looked in the mirror and said, "God made me this way, and I am fearfully and wonderfully made"?

Bald head, grey hair, red hair, whatever! No matter what we look like, God is the One behind us, so let's get involved with Him. The Psalmist David didn't say, "I wish I had dimples" or "Lord, I wish my nose was just a little bit shorter." No, David said, "I'm fearfully and wonderfully made."

Our God is a God of individuals. He knows who we are and what we look like, and yet some people try to tell God all the reasons why they can't do what He has destined them to do. When God taps them on the shoulder, they say, "Lord, I can't do what You want me to do. I'm this, that, and the other"—as if God didn't already know everything about them when He tapped them on the shoulder!

The Lord knew who He was tapping on the shoulder when He tapped you on the shoulder and said, "This is your destiny. This is what I want for you." He knew what He was doing!

Jeremiah 1:5 says, "Before I [God] formed you in the womb I knew you, before you were born I set you apart . . . " (*NIV*). God had a destiny and a purpose for Jeremiah's life before Jeremiah was ever born. I want you to understand that God has a destiny and a purpose for you too. God has placed you on the earth for such a time as this. God sent you His Word to tell you that He has formed and fashioned you for a specific purpose. You have a destiny; it's time to get up and get with it.

David

Everyone we read about in the Bible had a God-given destiny to fulfill. Adam was destined to be the father of mankind. Abraham was destined to be the father of many nations. Noah was destined to build the ark and thereby preserve a righteous remnant.

David's destiny wasn't only to kill Goliath or be a king. David's destiny was to be a praiser and a worshipper. The majority of the Book of Psalms was written as David praised and worshipped God. Perhaps the music didn't sound too good when David first started playing the harp out in the field while watching his father's sheep. But David was destined to play the harp to sooth Saul, the king of Israel. In First Samuel chapter 16, we read that when an evil spirit tormented King Saul, the king would summon David to come play the harp and drive the evil sprit away (1 Sam. 16:23). Yes, David was destined to be a praiser, but it was also destined that from his lineage would come, not a king, but the *King of kings*.

Of course, David probably couldn't comprehend the fullness of his destiny when he was still a shepherd out in the fields. And you may think you're out in the wilderness right now. You don't understand what God has planned for you. I'm sure David didn't understand what he was doing when he was just a kid watching the sheep. But friend, God had a destiny for him. And God has a destiny for you. Where you are now may not be where God has ultimately destined you to be. But if you can't learn to go through the place where you are now, you'll never reach the place where God has destined you to be.

Unfortunately, some people won't stay put long enough to learn anything or for God to show them anything.

Stay Put

I don't mean this to be derogatory in any way, but it wasn't always easy living in my father's and father-in-law's ministerial shadow. For years, everywhere I went I was introduced as Kenneth Hagin's son or V. E. Tipton's son-in-law. And much of the time, what I did in ministry wasn't in the public eye.

It can be frustrating to work behind the scenes, but I knew what God had told me to do. And I knew that if I was ever going to fulfill my God-given destiny and reach the place God wanted me to reach, I had to stay put!

Before you can do all God has destined you to do and before you can reach the place God wants you to reach, you're going to have to stay put and be faithful, even when it's not easy! But that's the way you get to your destiny—by being faithful where God plants you until He moves you somewhere else.

When my son told me that God had called him into the ministry, I didn't say anything to him right away, but I thought, *Oh, my. Both of his grandpas are all well-respected ministers and I'm in the ministry too. I sure hope he knows what he's getting into.* Since that time, I've watched Craig stay put and prove faithful. I watched him mow the grass on the RHEMA campus when he was the boss' son. I watched him work in the mechanics' shop changing oil in the ministry vehicles. From there, he moved to the shipping and receiving department, but he stayed at the ministry because he knew he had a destiny.

You may not especially enjoy where you are right now, but God may have you there for a reason. I didn't understand why I went through a lot of things at the time I was going through them. Looking back, I can see that God wanted me to learn some things so that I would be better prepared for where I am today. One good example of a preparation and learning period was the time I spent in the United States Army.

Preparation Time Isn't Wasted Time

During my senior year in college, I had a car accident and lost my military draft deferment. Soon after, I got a letter from Uncle Sam, saying "Congratulations! You are supposed to report to such and such place one month from now."

I didn't want to get drafted because I wanted to have some say in what I was assigned to do. So I went down and took a battery of tests, joined the Army, and went to work in communications.

During the three years I spent in the Army, I learned things that are helping me do what I'm doing today. One thing I learned was how to do one thing at a time, regardless of how many things I have to accomplish. Even with all the duties I have as Executive Vice-President of Kenneth Hagin Ministries and RHEMA Bible Training Center, Pastor of RHEMA Bible

Church, and International Director of RHEMA Ministerial Association International, I am still able to focus on one thing at a time and not be pressured or distracted by the other duties.

In the Army, I had to learn that when I walked out of the com center and shut the door behind me, I had to leave every part of my job there. I didn't take it with me; I didn't dare even talk about it. Now, when I walk out of my office at Kenneth Hagin Ministries, leaving a stack of papers on my desk, I never give it a thought. I am able to go preach and minister to people without thinking about the work I left behind, and when I get back to the office, I just pick up right where I left off.

People have asked me, "How are you able to do all that you do? How do you unhook from one thing and hook up to the other so well?" I learned those skills in the Army.

At the time I was in the Army, I didn't understand why I was there. I knew God had called me to be in full-time ministry, and I thought that being in the Army was way off course. You may be going down one road in life, but that doesn't mean your final destination is at the end of that road. The road you're on may lead somewhere unexpected, and the things you learn along the way will help you fulfill your ultimate destiny and purpose.

Be Faithful

Again, when I was going through different things at different times in my life, I didn't understand some of the reasons why. But I understand it all fully today. And because I was willing to stay put and be faithful in each instance, God was able to move me to the place in which I stand today.

I did what I had to do to fulfill my God-given destiny. You also have a destiny, but you're never going to fulfill it until you're willing to be faithful—until you're willing to sit down where you are and let God work with you until He gets ready to move you.

You might say, "You're talking about being in the ministry, but I'm not in the ministry."

I'm talking about ministry; I'm talking about secular work; I'm talking about wherever God has you.

You ask, "You mean God's interested in secular work?"

Of course He is! You ought to pray and find out exactly what area God wants you to be in. He has a destiny and a purpose especially for you.

God Means Business

Some people may not want to hear about staying put and being faithful. This is what I call a "meat and vegetables" message. If we have dessert all the time, we will become malnourished Christians. There are times we need to pull up to the table and eat some meat and vegetables.

Someone might say, "I don't like vegetables."

You might not like the way they taste, but they're good for you. You can't have a balanced diet or a healthy body without them.

Growing up, Mama always told us to eat our vegetables. When we asked her why, she said, "Because they're good for you." And when Mama said do it, we knew we better do it. I could always tell when my mama meant business.

The first time my mama would ask me to do something, she would say, "Ken, do such and such."

I'd say, "Okay, Mama," but then I would keep playing or doing whatever I was doing.

Then she'd said it again, "Ken, do such and such."

"Okay, Mama, I will in a minute."

Then I heard, "Kenneth *Wayne* . . . ," and before she could even get the "Hagin" out of her mouth, I was up and doing whatever she wanted me to do. I knew that when she said my whole name, Kenneth Wayne Hagin, she meant business! And I knew I better get up and get it done in a hurry! That wasn't the time to play around.

God may be calling you by your whole name. That means you better get busy. Friend, we are living in the last days, and God means business. This isn't the time to play around. When God tells you to do something, don't sit down on the couch and say, "Okay, God, in a minute." You have a destiny to fulfill. You are a part of God's plan, and He has a purpose for your life.

From the Pit to Prime Minister

Sometimes it may be hard to focus on the future or the dreams God has put in your heart, especially when the storms of life come against you. But remember, where you are right now is not where you will always be if you will stay confident that He " . . . who began a good work in you will carry it on to completion until the day of Christ Jesus" (Phil. 1:6 *NIV*).

Look at the life of Joseph. God took him from being a captive in a pit to being the prime minister of Egypt. Now, I'm not telling you to start believing God that you'll be thrown into a pit! All I'm saying is that God can take whatever situation you're in right now and turn it around to work out for your good (Rom. 8:28).

Joseph's brothers threw him in a pit and sold him as a slave. Joseph arrived in Egypt as a slave and later got thrown in jail. So far, it doesn't sound like Joseph's dream of stalks (his family) bowing down to him is going to come true (Gen. 37:5–8). It doesn't appear that he is going to be made ruler of anything.

Maybe right now you are going through some things, and your situation has you saying to yourself, *It doesn't look like I'm ever going to accomplish anything.* Just stay with God and He'll stay with you!

God brought Joseph out on the other side because Joseph stayed with Him. When Joseph could have gone the way of the world and probably stayed out of jail, Joseph stayed with God. And if you will stay with God and His Word even when it seems as though everything is going wrong, God will bring you out on the other side too!

Because Joseph chose to obey God and not defile himself with Potiphar's wife, he was thrown in jail. But he didn't stay in jail! When he was released, he became second in command of all Egypt and ended up with Pharaoh's ring on his finger. The only person in Egypt who had more power than he did was Pharaoh—the one who gave him the ring.

Joseph's steps were ordered of God even though it didn't look like they were. Often in Charismatic and "word of faith" circles, when we see something in our life that's not going quite right, we automatically think we missed it somewhere or that we're not in faith. Maybe we just need to keep following God.

Now don't misunderstand me. I'm not talking about going through life beaten down—poor, sick, and defeated. That's not what I'm talking about at all. I'm saying that as you're following God, you may get into some of these rough places. Some of these rough places may be where you find out if you have anything or not. Anyone can shout when everything is great. But can you shout and praise God when it's dark on every side and there's not a ray of light anywhere on the horizon?

Get Focused

We've read about several people in the Old Testament who fulfilled their destiny. Now let's look at two examples from the New Testament.

Mary had a destiny. Perhaps up until the time that the angel appeared to her, Mary had anticipated doing as she had always done. Of course, she planned on marrying Joseph and having a family, but then an angel appeared to her and said, "Mary, your destiny is to give birth to the Son of God."

John the Baptist also had a destiny. John lived out in the wilderness, dressed in camel's hair, and ate wild locusts and honey. To the world he looked and acted strange, but his destiny was to announce the coming of the Lord Jesus Christ.

Get focused on who you are, where you're going, and what you're supposed to be doing. Once you are on the path for your life, let nothing turn you aside.

Destiny Lost

There are many things in this world that will try to turn you aside from fulfilling your destiny. The Bible gives us many examples of people who were destined of God and then lost their destiny for one reason or another.

Originally Adam was destined to be keeper of the Garden, but when he disobeyed God, he lost his destiny and was driven out of the Garden. Many Christians today lose out because they quit following God.

Joseph could have lost his destiny if he hadn't said "no" to Potiphar's wife. Many people today lose their destiny when they don't say "no" to a situation that they should refuse. It doesn't even necessarily have to involve sin. For instance, a person might say "yes" to a business venture or job offer that he should refuse. By saying "yes," he misses the plan God had for him. Then he becomes frustrated because he's not fulfilling his destiny.

King Saul had a destiny as Israel's first king. When Samuel anointed Saul to be king, Saul was an humble man before God. But in the end, he made a wrong decision, lost his destiny, and took his own life by falling on his sword. The reason Saul lost his destiny didn't have anything to do with God; it had everything to do with Saul.

God is not to blame if we lose our destiny. Too many times, Christians want to blame the devil, the preacher, or someone else for the predicament they're in, when it's their own fault.

Saul did not have to lose his kingship, but he lost it through disobedience to God. Some people might not understand why Saul lost his kingdom because it seems that he did a good thing by sacrificing to God. But as discussed previously, although Saul did a right thing—offering a sacrifice to God—he did it the wrong way in disobedience to God.

God told Saul very specifically to do something, and Saul didn't do it. Saul became arrogant and willfully disobeyed God. He lost his destiny in doing what "appeared" to be right. God had commanded Saul and the people of Israel not to take any spoil from the enemy, but Saul disobeyed and brought back spoil.

When Samuel confronted him and reminded him of the Lord's command, Saul refused to take the blame and instead blamed his men. (Since when do the men rule the king?) So not only did Saul disobey, he also started lying and making excuses to the prophet of God! When you make a wrong move and get away from your destiny, it'll bring all kinds of junk into your life.

1 SAMUEL 15:13–16,19–23

13 When Samuel reached him [Saul], Saul said, "The Lord bless you! I have carried out the Lord's instructions."

14 But Samuel said, "What then is this bleating of sheep in my ears? What is this lowing of cattle that I hear?"

15 Saul answered, "The soldiers brought them from the Amalekites; they spared the best of the sheep and cattle to sacrifice to the Lord your God, but we totally destroyed the rest."

16 "Stop!" Samuel said to Saul. "Let me tell you what the Lord said to me last night." "Tell me," Saul replied. . . .

19 Why did you not obey the Lord? Why did you pounce on the plunder and do evil do evil in the eyes of the Lord?"

20 "But I did obey the Lord," Saul said. "I went on the mission the Lord assigned me. I completely destroyed the Amalekites and brought back Agag their king.

21 The soldiers took sheep and cattle from the plunder, the best of what was devoted to God, in order to sacrifice them to the Lord your God at Gilgal."

22 But Samuel replied: "Does the Lord delight in burnt

> offerings and sacrifices as much as in obeying the
> voice of the Lord? To obey is better than sacrifice, and
> to heed is better than the fat of rams.
> 23 For rebellion is like the sin of divination, and arrogance
> like the evil of idolatry. Because you have rejected the
> word of the Lord, he has rejected you as king."

Because of Saul's actions, he lost his destiny. God told him, "To *obey* Me is better than to sacrifice to Me." If we want to fulfill our destiny, we must obey the Lord at all times—obedience *is* better than sacrifice!

Don't Lose Out Over Money

Judas Iscariot is another example of someone who lost his destiny. Of the twelve disciples, Jesus chose Judas to be the treasurer, or keeper of the moneybag (John 13:29). Judas lost his destiny over money. And it wasn't just the thirty pieces of silver. That was the amount Judas betrayed Jesus for, but Judas had a problem with money long before the night he betrayed Jesus.

Remember when Mary brought the alabaster box of expensive perfume and poured it on Jesus (Matt. 26:7-9; John 12:3-7)? Judas said, "She shouldn't have wasted that. We could have sold the perfume and given the money to the poor." But Judas wasn't interested in the poor; he was interested in the money!

Don't misunderstand me. There's nothing wrong with having money, and there's nothing wrong with being prosperous, but we have to be careful that we don't get more interested in the money than in the things of God.

Many Christians today lose their destiny because of money. For instance, sometimes people lose their destiny because they take a job transfer without checking to see if the city they're moving to has a good church they can attend. The job transfer includes a big salary increase so they take it at the expense of their family's spiritual well-being. Making decisions based only on money can cause you to lose out on what God has for you.

Attitude Check

One very easy way to lose your destiny is to focus on everyone else's destiny. People who mind everyone else's business are usually depressed, irritable, and unhappy. Check your attitude right now. Are you always thinking that no one can do anything right? Are you always giving everyone a rough time? When problems come along, are they always someone else's fault?

The problem may not be with other people. It may be *you*! God wants you to focus on you and on your destiny. Remember God has a different plan for each of us, and it's important that we get on the course designed for us and stay on course!

Getting off course just a very little bit can change your whole direction. When flying an airplane, if the pilot gets off course just by two degrees, after two hours in the air he will be hundreds of miles off course. In life, you may start by getting just a little bit off course, but you can end up way off course.

If we don't continually keep readjusting and resetting ourselves according to the Word of God, we can get off course. And eventually, we will "crash and burn." But God will turn your direction around if you will listen to Him. He wants you to be happy and fulfilled in life, but that only happens when you stay on the course that He's destined for you.

In Numbers chapter 12, Miriam got out of her destiny when she and Aaron decided to tend to their brother Moses' business. As long as Miriam was doing what she was supposed to do with God (she was called to the position of helping Moses), she was okay. But when she tried to tend to *Moses'* business, she got leprosy. Fortunately for Miriam, Moses interceded with God on her behalf, and after a time of isolation according to the Levitical Law, she was healed of the leprosy.

Many people get out of the will of God and step out of their calling by trying to mind someone else's business. Do what God has called *you* to do. Fulfill *your* destiny. Accomplish what God has planned for *you* to do. And if you miss it and get off course, be quick to repent and get back on course.

Take Time to Pray

Discover God's destiny for your life. You are alive right now for a specific reason and purpose. Jeremiah 29:11 says, "'For I know the plans I have for you,' declares the Lord, 'plans to prosper you and not to harm you, plans to give you hope and a future'" (*NIV*) Take time to pray and seek God's direction, and He will reveal to you your specific destiny.

God has given a general destiny to every member of the Body of Christ, and that destiny is easily found in the Word of God. Reading the Word you discover that, as the song says, "We don't have to be sick no more! We don't have to be poor no more! We don't have to be bound no more by *anything*!"

You don't have to go through life living on "Barely-Get-Along Street" near "Grumble Alley" at "Thirty-third and Gone-Gone." You don't have to go through life with the soles of your shoes worn out, with the seat of your britches so thin you have to be careful not to rip them when you sit down, and wearing a hat with half a brim left because the dog chewed it. Some people think living that way is being humble. No, that's not being humble. Some people think being poor means you're holy. Poor is not holy!

The Word of God says we're supposed to be the head and not the tail, above and not beneath (Deut. 28:13). That's our destiny. If you are having financial problems right now, I want you to know because of what God has done through Jesus and because God has a destiny for you, you don't have to stay where you are. There's a way out. Your needs have been met according to His riches in glory (Phil. 4:19) and there is an abundant supply!

If you're in the place you're in because you missed it and stepped out of your destiny, just repent and get back on course. First John 1:9 says, *"If we confess our sins, he* [God] *is faithful and*

just to forgive us our sins, and to cleanse us from all unrighteousness."
God has a destiny for you to fulfill!

The Bible says that we can have life—spiritually, physically, mentally, emotionally, and so forth—and have it *more abundantly* (John 10:10)! God is interested in every part of our life—spirit, soul, and body. Third John 1:2 says, *"Beloved, I wish above all things that thou mayest prosper and be in health, even as thy soul prospereth."*

Some people say, "When we get to Heaven, everything's going to be great; it will be a happy day." Yes, Heaven's going to be great, but you don't have to wait until you get to Heaven to start enjoying life. The Word of God tells us that we can have a little bit of Heaven to go to Heaven with!

Go for the Gold!

You're not defeated. You're victorious. Romans 3:37 says we are more than conquerors. I like being a conqueror. A conqueror is the first-place winner!

Anyone who spends any time at all around me will discover that I don't have much use for second place. Usually, no one remembers who won the silver medal, so I always strive to win the gold. When I ran track in high school, I hated to receive the second-place medal. Second-place only meant that I wasn't fast enough to win the first-place medal.

Don't settle for second best with God. Remember, we're more than conquerors (Rom. 8:37), and in Christ, we are destined to win the gold.

Of course, in the natural we have to know how to lose graciously, but being a good sport doesn't mean we have to enjoy losing. In life, you cannot be defeated if you will not quit. If you quit, what are you going to win? But if you don't quit, what have you got to lose?

We are in a race. It's not a race to win a gold medal. It's a race for life or death. And in this race, we are more than conquerors through Jesus! Second Corinthians 2:14 says that we always triumph in Christ Jesus. It doesn't say we triumph *some* of the time or *part* of the time. It says we *always* triumph in Christ Jesus. That's our destiny. Our destiny is to always be triumphant.

It's time we begin to say, "I will not be defeated, and I will not quit. I am more than a conqueror. I cannot be defeated because the Word of God says that I always triumph in Christ Jesus. I'm not destined to be poor. I'm not destined to be defeated. I'm not destined to be sick. I am destined to be blessed, victorious, and healthy!"

Someone might ask, "Well, if Christians are not destined to be sick, why are so many of them sick?"

I don't know, but that doesn't change the fact that we're not destined to be sick. James 5:14 asks, "If there be any sick among you . . ." which indicates to me that there's not supposed to be any. But in case there are any sick among the brethren, James tells us what to do to get them healed.

Get excited about the future you're destined for. God has destined you for something other than being poor, defeated, and sick. I know that it's been preached that God wants you to be poor and sick, but that's man's theology, not God's. God said, "You don't have to be sick." God says, "You can be well, healthy, and whole."

Some have said, "Sickness is God's way of teaching you something." I never have found anyone who learned very much while they were sick. According to the way some people preach about our Heavenly Father's nature, if He were here on earth, He would be in court on trial for child abuse!

People say, "God made So-and-so sick. God did this; God did that." God didn't do it! Here's what God did: He sent Jesus Christ, His Son, to die on the Cross. Through Him, God destined you to be saved, healed, delivered, and set free!

Salvation, healing, and deliverance are only part of your destiny. Study God's Word and discover everything else that is part of your destiny.

The Time Is Now

Your destiny does not depend on God, it does not depend on Jesus, and it does not depend on any preacher. Your destiny does not depend on your spouse, on your mama and daddy, or on your grandma and grandpa. Your destiny and what you do with your life depends on *you*.

You can rise up, accept God's destiny, and begin to live the good life. Or you can sit down, enjoy being sick, poor, and defeated, and sing songs about "some day in Heaven."

Friend, make no mistake, "some day" is today! As I said in a previous chapter, "tomorrow" begins *today*! Don't misunderstand me—I'm not belittling what we will experience when we get to Heaven. But because of some of the teaching that says we have to wait until we get to Heaven to experience abundant life, the enemy has been robbing the Body of Christ of the destiny we are supposed to experience during our life here on earth.

Friend, you must realize that God has destined you for more than going through this life poor, sick, defeated, and without purpose. Find out what God has for you, then go out and possess it in the Name of Jesus.

I pray you will find God's destiny for you indelibly stamped upon your heart. And may God's purpose and plan for you change the way you live. I pray you will adjust yourself according to the Word so that you will discover your destiny—discover exactly what you're supposed to do in life—and then get in line with the vision God had placed within you.

If you receive the truths I have presented to you, and will walk in the light of what you have learned, you will be changed. You will also change your direction and begin to live the victorious life God wants you to live.

Make this statement of faith a continual confession of what you believe in your heart: "I cannot be defeated, and I will not quit. I don't have to be poor, because God has destined me for abundance. I don't have to be sick, because God has destined me for health. I don't have to be defeated, because God has destined me for victory. I accept all that God has destined for me. I will walk in my specific God-given destiny, and I will take my future by storm."

God has a *specific* plan for your life.
Are you ready?
RHEMA Bible Training Center

"... Giving all *diligence*, add to your faith *virtue*,
to virtue *knowledge* . . . .
For if these things are yours and *abound*,
you will be neither barren nor *unfruitful*
in the knowledge of our Lord Jesus Christ."
—2 Peter 1:5,8 (*NKJV*)

- Take your place in the Body of Christ for the last great revival.
- Learn to rightly divide God's Word and to hear His voice clearly.
- Discover how to be a willing vessel for God's glory.
- Receive practical hands-on ministry training from experienced ministers.

Qualified instructors are waiting to teach, train,
*and help **you** to fulfill your destiny!*

Call today for information or application material.
1-888-28-FAITH (1-888-283-2484)—Offer #P741
www.rbtc.org

RHEMA Bible Training Center admits students of any race, color, or ethnic origin.

Call now to receive a *free* subscription to *The Word of Faith* magazine from Kenneth Hagin Ministries. Receive encouragement and spiritual refreshment from . . .

FREE Subscription!

- *Faith-building articles from Rev. Kenneth Hagin Jr., Rev. Lynette Hagin, and others*

- *Timeless Teaching" from the archives of Rev. Kenneth E. Hagin*

- *Monthly features on prayer and healing*

- *Testimonies of salvation, healing, and deliverance*

- *Children's activity page*

- *Updates on RHEMA Bible Training Center, RHEMA Bible Church, and other outreaches of Kenneth Hagin Ministries*

Subscribe today!

1-888-28-FAITH (1-888-283-2484)

www.rhema.org/wof

Offer #P741

Correspondence Bible School

The RHEMA Correspondence Bible School is a home Bible study course that can help you in your everyday life!

This course of study has been designed with you in mind, providing practical teaching on prayer, faith, healing, Spirit-led living, and much more to help you live a victorious Christian life!

Flexible
Enroll any time: choose your topic of study; study at your own pace!

Affordable
Pay as you go—only $25 per lesson!
(Price subject to change without notice.)

Profitable

"Words cannot adequately describe the tremendous impact RCBS has had on my life. I have learned so much, and I am always sharing my newfound knowledge with everyone I can. I feel like a blind person who has just had his eyes opened!"

Louisiana

"RCBS has been a stepping-stone in my growing faith to serve God with the authority that He has given the Church over all the power of the enemy!"

New York

For enrollment information
and a course listing call today!

1-888-28-FAITH (1-888-283-2484)—Offer #P741

www.rhema.org/rcbs